The Scran Line

Sugar Rebels

Pipe for your life

NICK MAKRIDES

Hardie Grant
BOOKS

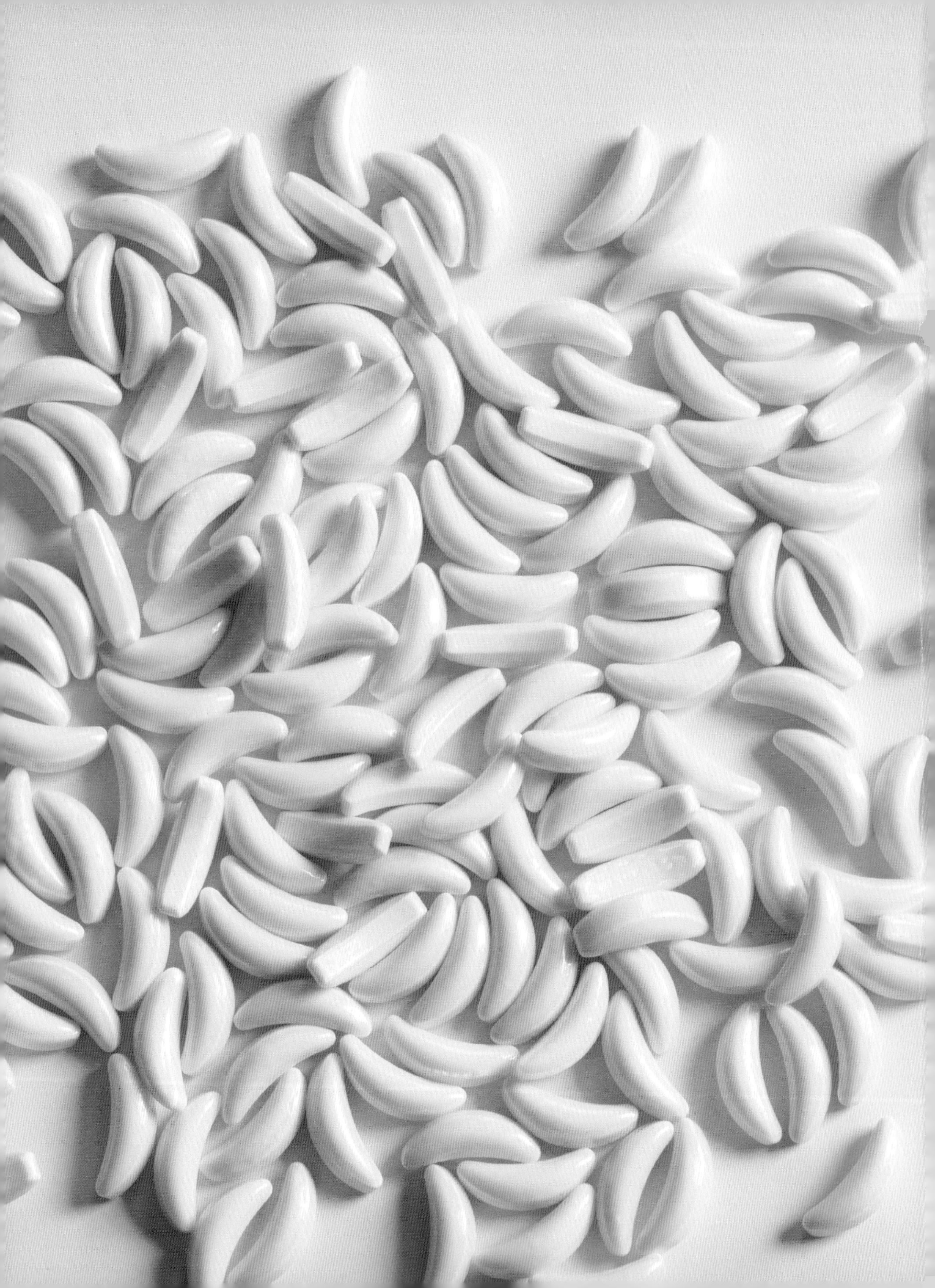

CONTENTS

INTRODUCTION 5

HOW TO USE THIS BOOK 6

BAKING TIPS & TRICKS 9

TOOLS & EQUIPMENT 21

–

REBEL BASICS 31

REBEL ALL-STARS 55

ERRYDAY REBEL 75

REBEL FREAK SHOW 113

REBEL THIRST QUENCHERS 129

REBEL PRIDE 147

REBEL KWEENS 165

REBELS REJOICE 189

–

INDEX 216

THANK YOU 219

THE THREE WISE WOMEN 222

INTRODUCTION

Before the health nuts start jumping up and down (and I love you guys BTW), *Sugar Rebels* is not my idea of rebelling against eating less sugar. We should definitely eat less sugar than we do now. Too much of anything is not good for you, especially sugar. Just ask the people who have to tan Donald Trump.

Sugar Rebels is a rebellion against what everyone else is doing with desserts. It's about using the things that inspire you to come up with original ideas for any dessert – in my case, cakes, cupcakes and macarons.

I've been doing social media for a long time. One of the challenges I faced from the very beginning was finding my own voice.

The number of times I've seen the same freaking unicorn cake on Instagram ... It makes me want to pull out what little hair I have left! Someone already made a unicorn cake with a gold fondant horn. There's no need for everyone to make it again and again until the internet is full of them. Be original. Create something new, something that is a part of you.

I want this book to inspire you to go into your kitchen and learn how to bake, but, more importantly, to get the creative juices flowing and make something that only *you* can make. Then jump on Instagram and share it with your followers – and me @thescranline!

N x

WHAT IS THE SCRAN LINE?

First of all, it's about me. I know that sounds super narcissistic, but let me explain ...

What makes you different from everyone else? List three things in your head. These differences are what makes people love you. Because you're you, and that's what they're drawn towards.

Same goes with The Scran Line. (And by the way, scran means food. That's the term used by the Royal Australian Navy. So, standing in the scran line means standing in the line for food.)

The Scran Line is about me. It's a personal online food project that stems from my love of design, baking and pop culture. I create video tutorials and post them on Facebook, YouTube and Instagram in an effort to inspire you guys to get in your kitchens and recreate them with your family and friends. I want you guys to learn a bunch of different techniques from my recipes, so that you can then begin creating your own designs based on the things that inspire you.

For me, it's my love of pop culture and music, as well as my passions for design and creating pastries. These are some of the biggest things that make me who I am.

The Scran Line is my way of sharing all of those things with you guys. It's my creative outlet, it's how I communicate and connect with people. You know how Beyoncé literally does no interviews and the only way we found out about Becky with the good hair was through her music? Music is the way Beyoncé expresses who she is.

The Scran Line is my way of expressing who I am.

HOW TO USE THIS BOOK

This book isn't your run-of-the-mill recipe book. You can't pick a recipe to make in 40 minutes on a weekday. These are recipes you take time to make over the weekend with friends and family. They are designed to teach you different techniques in the kitchen.

Sugar Rebels is my way of encouraging you to get in the kitchen and have fun baking on your own or with someone else. I want you guys to experience the same things I experienced in my mum and grandma's kitchens: spending time with family and friends baking something delicious while you laugh, make mistakes, argue and then finish it all off by eating something amazing.

Each recipe is adapted from one of the base recipes in the Rebel Basics chapter (page 31).

So, let's say you've decided to make the Highway unicorn cake (page 70). That cake is based on my Vanilla cake recipe (page 37), which is located in the Rebel Basics chapter. Start off by reading the base recipe, then read the recipe that you've chosen. Once you've got an understanding of the ingredients and steps in both recipes, you're ready to begin.

I decided to structure the book this way to avoid giving you the exact same ingredients list and instructions in every recipe. You're welcome, forests!

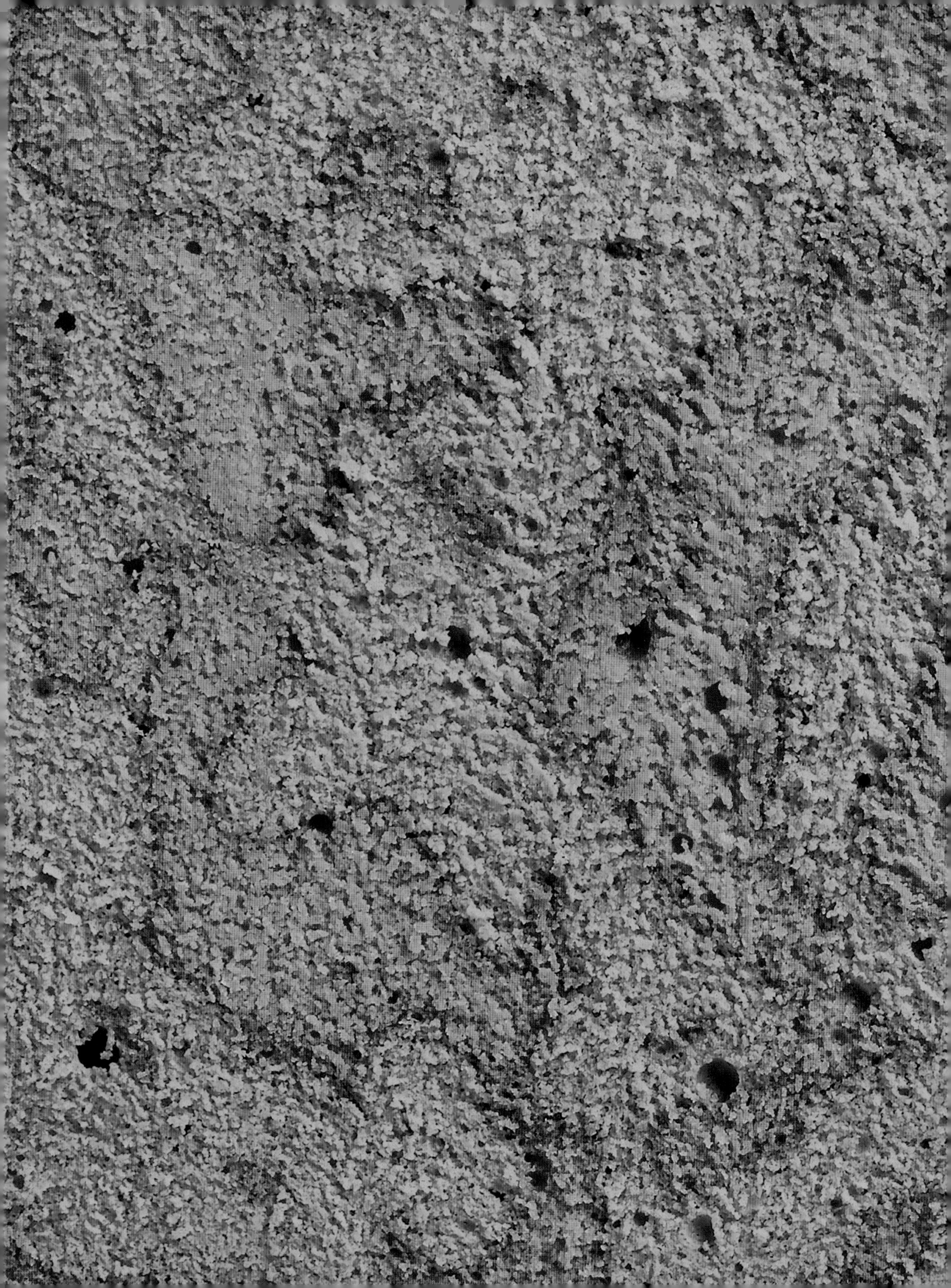

BAKING TIPS & TRICKS

Here's some extra info that will come in handy for the recipes in this book.

USING KITCHEN SCALES

Guys, I just cannot stress enough how important it is to measure everything out correctly and precisely when you're baking. Especially for macarons. The reason is that there is a lot of science behind baking and how all the different ingredients work together. For example, did you know that every egg is a different size? You might be thinking: 'What on earth is Nick saying? Of course I know that!' Some people don't actually realise it though. The questions I've had over the years, you wouldn't even believe. For macarons, it's impossible to say use '4 egg whites', because you're going to get a different amount of egg whites every time depending on the size of the eggs. So, what I would recommend is that you invest in a pair of kitchen scales. Make sure they're digital and don't have a touch-button. Touch-button scales are kind of flaky, no matter how much they might cost. When you switch between bowls of different ingredients and want to set the scale back to zero, you want to be able to *feel* that you pressed the button and are sure that it registered. The ones with actual buttons are always better.

The other thing I would recommend is that you read the recipe thoroughly first and make sure you have all the correct ingredients measured out accurately before you start. Some recipes have steps where multiple things need to happen at once, so you won't have time to pause and measure out ingredients.

So, the key takeaways are: a pair of good kitchen scales is a worthwhile investment, always measure accurately, and measure before you begin a recipe.

CAKES & CUPCAKES

A TWO-DAY PROCESS

All the cakes in this book take two days to make. Aim to bake the cakes on day one, then trim, fill, crumb-coat (page 10) and decorate on day two.

USING YOGHURT

First of all, no, you can't taste it – it's such a small amount. Sorry for all of you yoghurt lovers out there. The addition of yoghurt to my Vanilla cupcakes (page 34) and cake recipes keeps the cakes moist. This is especially important for a couple of reasons. If you're baking your cupcakes the night before a party, then the yoghurt will help keep the cupcakes and cakes moist until the next day. The reason it's not an ingredient in the chocolate recipes is that these recipes use much more butter, so the butter helps keep the cake moist. You can use sour cream instead of yoghurt – it does the same thing.

HALVING THE RECIPE

My Chocolate cake (page 41), Chocolate cupcakes (page 38), Vanilla cake (page 37) and Vanilla cupcakes (page 34) can be halved by simply halving the ingredients. My Red velvet cupcakes recipe (page 33) cannot be halved. I'd recommend just making the whole batch and sharing them with your neighbours, family and friends if you want to avoid eating all the yumminess yourself!

BUTTER

Make sure your butter is very soft for the cake mixture. There are two ways to soften your butter. You can microwave it (as one whole block) for 5 seconds at a time, flipping the block over halfway through, until very soft (not melted). If you don't have a microwave, run a large bowl under hot water. Dry the bowl and place it over the butter for 1 minute. The heat from the bowl will create a warm environment within to soften the butter.

HAND MIXER

Cupcakes and cakes can be mixed using a hand mixer (always on the lowest speed) or a hand whisk. Take care not to overmix the batter.

PREPARING YOUR CAKE TIN
For the cake recipes, you'll need at least one 20 cm (8 in) cake tin, but preferably three 20 cm (8 in) cake tins. To prepare the tin, spray with oil spray. To prepare the baking paper, place the cake tin on a sheet of baking paper and use a pen to trace around the bottom of the tin. Use scissors to cut out the baking paper, slightly inside the circle you traced. Place in the cake tin and you're good to go! Personally, I prefer not to line the sides of my cake tins. Once a cake has baked and cooled, just run a knife around the edge and it should come out easily.

OVEN TEMPERATURE
Each oven is different. Some are old, some are new. Some ovens can be hotter on the inside than the temperature you set it at. If you find your cupcakes, cakes or macarons are browning or cracking, turn the oven down 10°C (50°F). A handy trick is to use an oven thermometer, which sits inside the oven and gives an accurate temperature reading. They're inexpensive and can be bought online or at your local kitchen supply store. Always bake on the middle rack of the oven for the best results.

BAKING TIME
The baking time for each cupcake or cake may vary depending on your oven or the recipe. Some people's ovens run hotter than others, so it's important to get to know yours when making desserts. I bake my cupcakes on a low temperature at a slower rate than others do. There are a couple of reasons for this. It ensures I get a nice flat top on my cakes and cupcakes, with no cracks – the lower temperature allows them to rise nice and slowly and hold their shape. It also helps to keep coloured cakes nice and bright and stops them from going weird, dull colours.

For cakes, stick a skewer into the centre of the cake after 50 minutes. If it comes out coated in wet batter, bake for another 10 minutes, or until the skewer comes out clean or with a few crumbs. For cupcakes, do the same at the 40-minute mark. Some cakes or cupcakes can take longer to bake (such as those with fresh berries, which release extra moisture), so allow for extra baking time with these. What I'd encourage you to do is experiment with your oven and pay close attention to the temperature settings. If things are baking too quickly and drying out, lower the temperature. If things are taking too long to bake, raise the temperature by about 10°C (50°F).

STORAGE
Refrigerate in an airtight container for up to 3 days (remove from the fridge 1 hour before serving and leave to come to room temperature).

TRIMMING, FILLING AND CRUMB-COATING CAKES

A double batch of my Vanilla cake (page 37) and Chocolate cake (page 41) dough makes three 20 cm (8 in) cakes. Once cut horizontally in half, you will end up with six layers of cake from each recipe.

To trim your chilled cakes, use a cake leveller (see page 26) or a large, serrated knife to carefully trim the crusts off the top of the cakes before cutting each cake in half to make the six layers. You will need half of the recipe's frosting quantity for the crumb-coat stage.

To prepare the crumb coat, add a dab of frosting to the middle of a 20 cm (8 in) cake board or serving plate. Use a small offset spatula (see page 21) to spread it around a little before topping with the first cake layer. Gently press down on the cake to make sure it's stuck to the cake board.

Add the frosting to a piping bag and snip off the end. Pipe a ring of frosting around the top of the cake layer, then fill the middle with more frosting. Smooth it out with the spatula before adding the next cake layer. Repeat with the remaining layers until all six have been used (use about half of the crumb-coat frosting for the layering stage).

Use the remaining frosting to coat the top and side of the cake. I usually pipe the frosting in a zig-zag pattern around the side of the cake and pipe a dollop on top. This helps to distribute the frosting more evenly. Use the spatula to smooth it out, taking care to fill in any gaps in between the cake layers.

Use a cake scraper (otherwise known as a bench scraper; see page 26) to smooth out the frosting on the side and top, getting it as neat as you can. This is just a thin layer of frosting aimed at trapping any cake crumbs so that random bits of crumb don't show up in the final layer of frosting (hence the term crumb-coating). Chill, uncovered, for 2 hours or overnight.

Your cake is now crumb-coated! You can leave it as is – a 'naked' cake – and top with decorations, or add another layer of frosting for a smoother finish.

FROSTING A CAKE

Once the cake has been crumb-coated and chilled (page 10), you can add a final layer of frosting. Use the other half of the recipe's frosting quantity for this second frosting layer.

Pipe your frosting onto the cake, starting at the bottom then working your way around until you reach the top. Use a large cake scraper (page 26) to scrape the side and top of the cake until they're smooth. A turntable (page 26) is very helpful for this step, as it enables you to spin the cake while you hold the cake scraper against the cake with your other hand.

FROSTING TIPS & TRICKS

ADDING COLOUR AND FLAVOUR

Frosting should be coloured using food-gel colouring only, not liquid food dye. To colour, add the desired amount of food-gel colouring and use a hand whisk or a stand mixer fitted with the paddle attachment (for American buttercream frosting) or the whisk attachment (for Swiss meringue buttercream frosting) to incorporate the colour into the frosting. The same goes with food flavourings. Food gels and flavourings can go in at the point where you'd add the vanilla extract/bean paste or cocoa powder.

AMERICAN BUTTERCREAM FROSTING

MILK

The small addition of full-cream (whole) milk to my American buttercream frosting recipe (page 45) serves a couple of purposes: it helps to smooth out the frosting and makes the sugar less grainy. It also makes the buttercream fluffier. Generally, you should add the milk as it makes the frosting much nicer, but don't be tempted to add too much, otherwise it will split. The only time I wouldn't recommend adding the milk is on warm days, as it will make the frosting very soft and it won't hold its shape.

STORAGE/MAKING IT IN ADVANCE

You can make your buttercream up to 2 weeks before you need it. Simply store in the refrigerator in an airtight container. To freshen it up, remove from the refrigerator and set aside for 1 hour to come to room temperature. Whip the buttercream again on high speed for 10 minutes using a hand mixer or a stand mixer until it's fluffy and pale in colour.

SWISS MERINGUE BUTTERCREAM FROSTING

Swiss meringue buttercream (page 46) is a great alternative for those who want a smoother, shinier-looking buttercream. First, it is sweetened by creating a Swiss meringue, then butter is added to the meringue to turn it into a silky-smooth buttercream, making it perfect for smooth-looking cakes.

SMOOTH FROSTING

If you find your frosting is too aerated (has too many air bubbles), mix it in your stand mixer on the lowest speed for about 10 minutes and it will become perfectly smooth.

STORAGE/MAKING IT IN ADVANCE

You can make your Swiss meringue frosting up to two weeks before you need it. Simply store in the fridge in an airtight container. To freshen it up, remove the container from the fridge and set aside for 1 hour to come to room temperature. Whip the frosting again on high speed for 10 minutes using a hand mixer or a stand mixer until it's fluffy and pale in colour. For really silky-smooth frosting, mix for another 10 minutes on the lowest speed.

CREAM CHEESE FROSTING

MIXING SPEED

Make sure that you ALWAYS mix this frosting (page 47) on high speed. The only point at which you want to mix on low speed is when the dry ingredients have been added. As soon as they have been incorporated, turn the mixer up to high speed until everything is well combined and you're left with a pale, fluffy frosting.

STORAGE/MAKING IT IN ADVANCE

I wouldn't recommend making this frosting too far in advance. It tastes and looks better when fresh. You can make it the day before, and re-whip it to freshen it up. Simply remove it from the refrigerator and set aside for 30 minutes to come to room temperature. Whip the frosting again on high speed for 10 minutes using a hand mixer or a stand mixer until it's fluffy and pale in colour. Remember, ALWAYS mix this frosting on high speed to avoid it softening too much.

DOS AND DON'TS

Guys, I cannot stress enough how important it is to whip this delicious frosting on high speed. Always use food flavourings to flavour your cream cheese frosting. Avoid adding fresh or frozen fruit, as the excess liquid will cause the frosting to soften. A good alternative is freeze-dried fruit. Just crush it into a powder before adding it with the icing (confectioners') sugar and milk powder.

HOW TO PIPE LIKE A PRO

There are two types of people in this world: people who are naturals at frosting cupcakes perfectly, and people who need practice. For most people, it's not something you are born being able to do, but it is something you can learn by practising. I first learned how to pipe frosting on a cupcake properly at my first bakery job. After about two weeks of piping every day, I became a pro. For me, it was definitely all about practice.

If you're someone who needs practice and guidance, here are my top three piping tips and some of the frosting styles I use in this book. Let's begin!

1. FITTING THE END OF A PIPING BAG WITH A PIPING TIP
There are two types of piping bags you can use: disposable plastic piping bags, and reusable cloth piping bags. I tend to use disposable ones because there's no cleaning up and they just go in the recycling bin when you're finished. They're also easier to use as you can cut whatever size hole you need to fit either small or large piping tips. With reusable bags, you're kind of stuck with that one-sized cut at the end of the bag.

To see all the piping tips I use in this book, take a look at my Tools & Equipment section (page 22). To fit the end of your piping bag with a tip, place the piping tip inside the bag, pushing it into the corner. Make a mental note of where to cut. You want to cut the piping bag so that it exposes only half of the tip. Take the tip out, cut the corner of the bag and put your tip back in, pushing it through the hole you've just made.

2. FILLING A PIPING BAG
Most people can fill a piping bag by holding it in one hand and scooping the frosting into the bag using a spatula. But, if you're a beginner, an easy way to fill a piping bag is to put your piping bag (with the tip fitted) into a tall glass. Fold the top of the piping bag over the sides of the glass and add your frosting. Fill the bag up just over halfway, then twist the end.

3. HOLDING A PIPING BAG
The most important thing to do when frosting your cupcakes is to hold your piping bag straight. You can pipe with one hand, but I'd recommend using both hands if you're a beginner. Bend the twisted part of the piping bag over and use whichever hand you write with to cup the top of the piping bag like you would a tennis ball. This is the hand you'll use to squeeze out the frosting. You'll use the other hand as a guide while you pipe. Don't use the guiding hand to squeeze the frosting, otherwise your frosting will come spilling out the top of the bag.

MY FAVE FROSTING STYLES

1. SIGNATURE SWIRL
For this technique, you'll need a Wilton 1M piping tip. Starting in the centre of the cupcake, pipe a swirl of frosting about 1 cm (½ in) from the edge of the cupcake. Continue swirling upwards and inwards until you get to the top. Pipe slowly to allow the frosting to come out looking frilly. When you reach the top, stop squeezing, then lift up the piping bag to get that perfect little pointy tip in the middle.

I use this technique for my classic-looking and simple cupcakes. It's such a gorgeous technique, it just needs a simple-flavoured cupcake.

2. ROUND BULB
For this technique, you'll need a round piping tip. Begin in the centre of the cupcake. Hold the tip about 1 cm (½ in) away from the surface of the cake and squeeze out a bulb of frosting in a single motion. If you want a taller bulb, slightly lift the piping bag as you squeeze to give the bulb more height. To get a flat bulb, hold the piping tip closer to the cupcake. You can also pipe little bulbs on top of one large bulb.

I use this technique for simple cupcakes, or for when I want to coat the frosting in something crumbly, like crushed cookies, as the bulb shape helps to hold the toppings in place.

3. SOFT-SERVE SWIRL
You can use any piping tip for this technique, but to get that soft-serve ice-cream look, use an open star tip. Starting in the centre of the cupcake, pipe a swirl of frosting about 1 cm (½ in) from the edge of the cupcake. Continue swirling upwards and inwards until you get to the top. When you reach the top, stop squeezing and lift up the piping bag to get that perfect little pointy tip.

This is a really versatile and classic technique that is used on most cupcakes.

4. DOUBLE-DOUGHNUT SWIRL
You can use any piping tip for this technique. Starting in the centre of the cupcake, pipe a swirl of frosting about 1 cm (½ in) from the edge of the cupcake, then pipe a second circle of frosting directly on top of the bottom circle, using the bottom swirl as a guide to getting them even.

This frosting technique is great for piling on decorations because the cupcake has a flat surface area in the middle. You can drizzle some sauce over it too, just like you would on top of a cake.

2
3
4

HOW TO CREATE DRIPS

Guys, this is all about consistency! To create drips, use freshly made Chocolate sauce (page 51) – it has the perfect drip consistency. To bring back sauce that has set, microwave for 20 seconds at a time until a drop applied to your finger drips down (but make sure it does not become translucent).

To add drips to your cake, add the sauce to a squeeze bottle. You may have to enlarge the hole in the nozzle for better flow. Hold the bottle firmly, then squeeze around the cake as you slowly turn the cake on a turntable. The longer you stop and squeeze on the edge of the cake, the longer the drip will be. You don't want all your drips to be the same length – make some shorter, others longer.

HOW TO CUT CAKE

This is one of the most common questions I get! There are lots of different ways to cut a cake, but this is one of the easiest methods, and one of the best ways to ensure everyone gets equal amounts of cake and frosting. There's nothing worse than having just cake and not enough yummy frosting!

You won't be cutting the cake in wedges. Instead, you'll be taking a large slice off the side of the cake. Place a chopping board upright against the slice and use the knife to guide the cake slice onto the chopping board, then bring the board down onto your workbench. Next, proceed to cut the cake into vertical strips, then cut those in half. Repeat until the entire cake is cut. Quick and easy!

MACARONS

PREPARE BEFORE YOU START

1. Trays – lined with baking paper not greaseproof paper.
2. Eggs – separate the egg whites from the yolks and refrigerate for a couple of hours. These must be measured accurately (see page 42).
3. Sifting – sift the almond flour and sugar together. If you're combining your almonds and sugar using a food processor, sift the mixture once after blitzing. If you're not using a food processor, sift the mixture three times to remove any big lumps of almond flour.

ALMOND FLOUR VS ALMOND MEAL

Almond meal and almond flour are basically the same thing. They're both finely ground almonds. The only difference is that almond flour uses blanched ground almonds, that is, skinless almonds, whereas almond meal can be either blanched or unblanched. Blanched almond flour will be a creamy white flour, whereas almond meal will contain flecks of brown from the almond skins. For macarons, you want to make sure you used blanched almonds so that you can get those bright colours. And no, you can't replace almond flour with plain (all-purpose) flour. The recipe just won't work. In fact, none of the ingredients in my macaron recipes should be replaced. You must be super accurate.

AGEING YOUR EGGS

Try to steer away from using freshly laid eggs for macarons because they don't whip up as easily as store-bought eggs. If you want to get the best results, separate your egg whites from their yolks and refrigerate the whites for several days, preferably a week (make sure to keep them covered to avoid contamination). This process is known as 'liquefying'. During this time, the albumen (egg whites) lose their elasticity and break down, which makes them much easier to whisk to soft peaks without turning 'grainy'.

HALVING THE RECIPE

This recipe can be halved by simply halving the ingredients.

STORAGE

Store in an airtight container for up to 3 days (refrigerated or unrefrigerated). After that they will start to soften or dry out depending on the humidity in the air.

EQUIPMENT

I have dedicated baking trays for macarons because I like to keep them perfectly clean and flat. Flat baking trays are super important for getting your macarons to rise perfectly every time, so make sure you don't dent or warp them by putting a heavy roast on them or something. It might seem excessive, but I do what I can to make sure my macarons turn our perfectly every time, and flat baking trays are key!

To line your trays, always use baking paper, not greaseproof paper. An even better and more environmentally friendly option is to use silicone baking mats. You can find these at your local kitchen supply store. Just make sure you measure your trays before you get them to ensure they will fit perfectly and don't overhang the sides. Again, the mats have to lay flat on the baking trays for your macarons to rise properly.

CARTON EGG WHITES

'Hey Nick, can I use carton eg...' I'm gonna stop you right there and say no! They're not cheaper and it's always better to use real, fresh ingredients. Remember, stick to the ingredients in my macaron recipes if you want to recreate them exactly.

USING A SUGAR THERMOMETER

So, sugar thermometers come in really handy for lots of different things, but you'll need one for my macaron recipes. They can cost anywhere between $20–$100 and you can use them for lots of different recipes. Can you make macarons without one? Yeah, technically you can, and there are guides online for testing the different stages of making the syrup, but, in my opinion, it's just easier to buy a sugar thermometer. You'll get a lot of use out of it and using a thermometer removes the guesswork when making things like syrups.

COLOURING YOUR MACARONS

To colour your macarons, use food-gel colouring only. Liquid food dye will add too much moisture to your macarons, which can cause them to crack when baking.

RIBBON STAGE

Mixing your macaron batter, otherwise known as 'macaronage', is really important. A lot of people like to count the number of times they mix. I think that's silly. I think it's better to know what consistency to look out for when mixing your batter. The way I like to mix mine is by going around the bowl with a spatula and then through the middle. This slightly deflates the air in the mixture, allowing you to thin out the batter. You'll know when to stop when you reach the 'ribbon stage'. The ribbon stage is when the batter falls off the spatula in a ribbon when you hold it up, before disappearing back into the batter in the bowl after about 10 seconds. While you're mixing, and when you think you're nearing that stage, start testing the batter for that ribbon consistency. As you get closer, you'll need to mix less and less. When you reach that magic stage, stop mixing immediately. If you continue mixing beyond the ribbon stage, you'll thin out the batter too much and that causes a whole heap of problems. If you don't get it right the first time, don't stress, it can take a bit of practice.

MACARON TROUBLESHOOTING

MY MERINGUE WON'T BEAT TO STIFF PEAKS

There may be oil residue on your bowl. Make sure you use a very clean glass or metal bowl only, not plastic. A great way to make sure you get rid of any oil on your bowl is to lightly wipe it down with a paper towel dipped in a little white vinegar.

MY MACARON BATTER IS TOO RUNNY

- Make sure you beat your meringues to stiff peaks. Sometimes you may need to whip them a little longer than what the recipe says. Just always make sure that the meringue is at stiff peaks before it goes into the almond mixture. To test for stiff peaks, carefully run a spatula through your egg whites to create a peak in the bowl, then make a peak on the spatula itself. If the peaks hold their shape and the egg white does not fall off the spatula when turned over, the meringue is ready. If the peaks collapse, keep whisking.
- The most likely thing that's happened is you've overmixed your batter. Be really careful when mixing; it's where most people go wrong. Go around the bowl with a spatula and then through the middle. Continue mixing until you reach the 'ribbon stage' (see above). Unfortunately, if you have overmixed your batter, there is no way to fix this and you will have to start again.

MY MACARONS HAVE PEAKS ON THEM THAT WON'T GO AWAY

You haven't mixed the batter enough.

MY SHELLS HAVE CRACKED IN THE OVEN

- You may not have mixed the almond mixture in with the meringue well enough.
- The oven temperature may have been too high. Try lowering it by about 10°C (50°F).
- Make sure you use baking paper not greaseproof paper. Greaseproof paper can cause your macaron shells to crack.

MY MACARON FEET ARE UNEVEN AND MY MACARONS AREN'T RISING ENOUGH

- The oven temperature may be too low. Increase the temperature by 10°C (50°F).
- You may have handled the trays roughly, which can cause the shells to tilt when they rise. Try not to bump the trays and make sure they're set on an even surface while the macarons are drying.

WHY ARE MY SHELLS HOLLOW?

- You may have overbeaten your egg whites and incorporated too much air.
- Your oven temperature may be too high, which can cause the shells to rise too quickly. Try lowering the temperature by 10°C (50°F), see how the next batch goes and adjust again if needed. A lower, slower temperature will help them rise nice and evenly and not dry out.

WHY WON'T MY MACARONS COME OFF THE TRAY?

- It's probably because they're undercooked. Try baking them for a little longer or raising your oven temperature by 10°C (50°F).
- The shells may not have cooled down fully. Make sure your shells are completely cool before taking them off the tray.

Breville
KENWOOD
KENWOOD

TOOLS & EQUIPMENT

Guys, before I get into this, you don't have to have everything on this list to be able to make great cakes, cupcakes or macarons. These are things that I have accumulated over the years as my passion for baking grew. In this section, I wanted to share some of the things I feel are important in helping me create the cakes that I do!

N x

MEASURING TOOLS

- My kitchen scales: Breville BSK 500 max load 5 kg (11 lb)
- Measuring spoons
- Measuring cups: in various sizes – 250 ml (8½ fl oz/1 cup), 125 ml (4 fl oz/½ cup), 80 ml (2½ fl oz/⅓ cup) and 60 ml (2 fl oz/¼ cup)

STAND MIXER

OK, so this part is in no way sponsored by Kenwood, but I love my Kenwood machine. In fact, I was so excited to get it that I asked you guys to come up with a name for it and, lo and behold, my mixer is named Peggy. Peggy is my best friend in the kitchen. She helps me with most things, like making frosting, batter and meringues.

Now guys, a lot of people swear by their KitchenAid mixers, and I get a lot of questions about why I use a Kenwood machine instead of a KitchenAid. I own and have used a KitchenAid but, personally, I find Kenwood machines are able to handle everything. They're powerful enough for me to use on a hard dough without having to worry that they'll break. They're also a little cheaper. But, at the end of the day, they both mix well and everyone has their personal preference.

- Peggy the stand mixer: Kenwood Chef Sense Stand Mixer KVL6100G Chef Sense 4.6Ltr green with glass bowl. Peggy comes with a paddle, whisk and dough hook attachment. She also came with a bunch of other cool attachments. When you're choosing a stand mixer, don't go with a cheaper brand. Go with a well-trusted brand. The ones that are a little more expensive last for decades and the last thing you want is your mixer pooping itself in the middle of making a beautiful glossy meringue!
- Paddle attachment: Used for making batters and American buttercream frosting (page 45).
- Whisk attachment: Used mostly for making meringues and Swiss meringue buttercream frosting (page 46).
- Dough hook: You won't see me using this very much, but I use it very occasionally when I make doughnuts or bread.

HAND MIXER & FOOD PROCESSOR

I would use Peggy to help me make everything, but I soon realised that not everyone has a stand mixer like Peggy, so I switched to making all of my batters with my trusty hand mixer, Bruce.

- Bruce the hand mixer: Braun MultiMix 3 hand mixer
- Food processor: Kenwood Multipro Classic Food Processor FDM785BA. I mostly use this for my macaron recipes to help combine the almond flour and icing (confectioners') sugar. This machine can be used for lots of different things, but it's not absolutely vital to have one.

SPATULAS

- Large spatula: Here's what you want to look for in a spatula, because there are a lot of bad spatulas out there. Ideally you want something very strong, something that's one-piece, with a firm rubber bit at the end that is still slightly bendy. A spatula that is too bendy is difficult to use, especially on something like folding macaron batter. You need something firm for that and for scraping down batters and frosting. I use a Pyrex, 30 cm (12 in) high × 6.5 cm (2½ in) wide.
- Large offset spatula: I use this for transferring my cake from the cake turntable to the fridge.
- Small offset spatula: I use this when frosting my cakes to help smooth out the crumb-coat.

ICE-CREAM SCOOPS

I use the medium scoop for most of my videos unless I tell you guys to scoop differently. Don't ask me what brands they are, as I've had them for ages. I bought two from a store in Melbourne and the little one is from eBay. When you're buying a scoop, be careful; the cheap ones won't last long, so try to see buying a good scoop as an investment.

- Large scoop: 6.5 cm (2½ in) bowl diameter
- Medium scoop: 5.5 cm (2¼ in) bowl diameter
- Small scoop: 4 cm (1½ in) bowl diameter

PIPING TIPS

So, I use a lot of piping tips. In fact, I have about 100 of them. Some are duplicates for when I use different-coloured frostings on one cake or macaron. Here's my advice for people starting out: get five piping tips – Wilton 1M; Wilton 6B; a large round tip; a medium round tip, and an open-star tip. You can do a lot of different things with just those five tips.

You can buy piping tips online or at your local cake decorating or craft store. They're super cheap too. Don't buy kits. Kits are full of tips you'll never use. Buy the ones you need, and make sure they're good-quality. And before anyone asks, yes, I have tried Russian piping tips. I've even made a video about them ... I'm not a fan. I think they're lazy and harder to use than regular piping tips. You get better results with the regular tips like the ones listed below.

- Wilton 8B tip: Used for cupcakes and cakes.
- Wilton 6B tip: Used for macarons.
- Wilton #32 tip: Used for macarons.
- Wilton 1M tip: Used for cakes, cupcakes and macarons. I use this tip to get my signature frilly swirl frosting.
- Wilton #4 tip: Used for small details, such as for my Lemonade cake (page 181).
- Small round tip: 1 cm (0.4 in) in diameter
- Medium round tip: Ateco #11, 1.4 cm (0.5 in) in diameter
- Large round tip: Ateco #13, 1.6 cm (0.6 in) in diameter
- Open-star tip: Ateco #11
- Grass tip

PIPING BAGS

- Medium piping bag: 30 cm (12 in)
- Large piping bag: 40 cm (15.5 in)

MOULDS

- Half-silicone mould: 5 cm (2 in) high × 6.5 cm (2½ in) wide
- Jewel moulds: Grainrain Round Diamond-Shaped Chocolate Candy Mould Polycarbonate PC DIY Mould
- Martellato Polycarbonate Chocolate Mould Half-Sphere 10 cm (4 in), 2 cavities
- Martellato Polycarbonate Chocolate Mould Half-Sphere 5 cm (2 in), 8 cavities

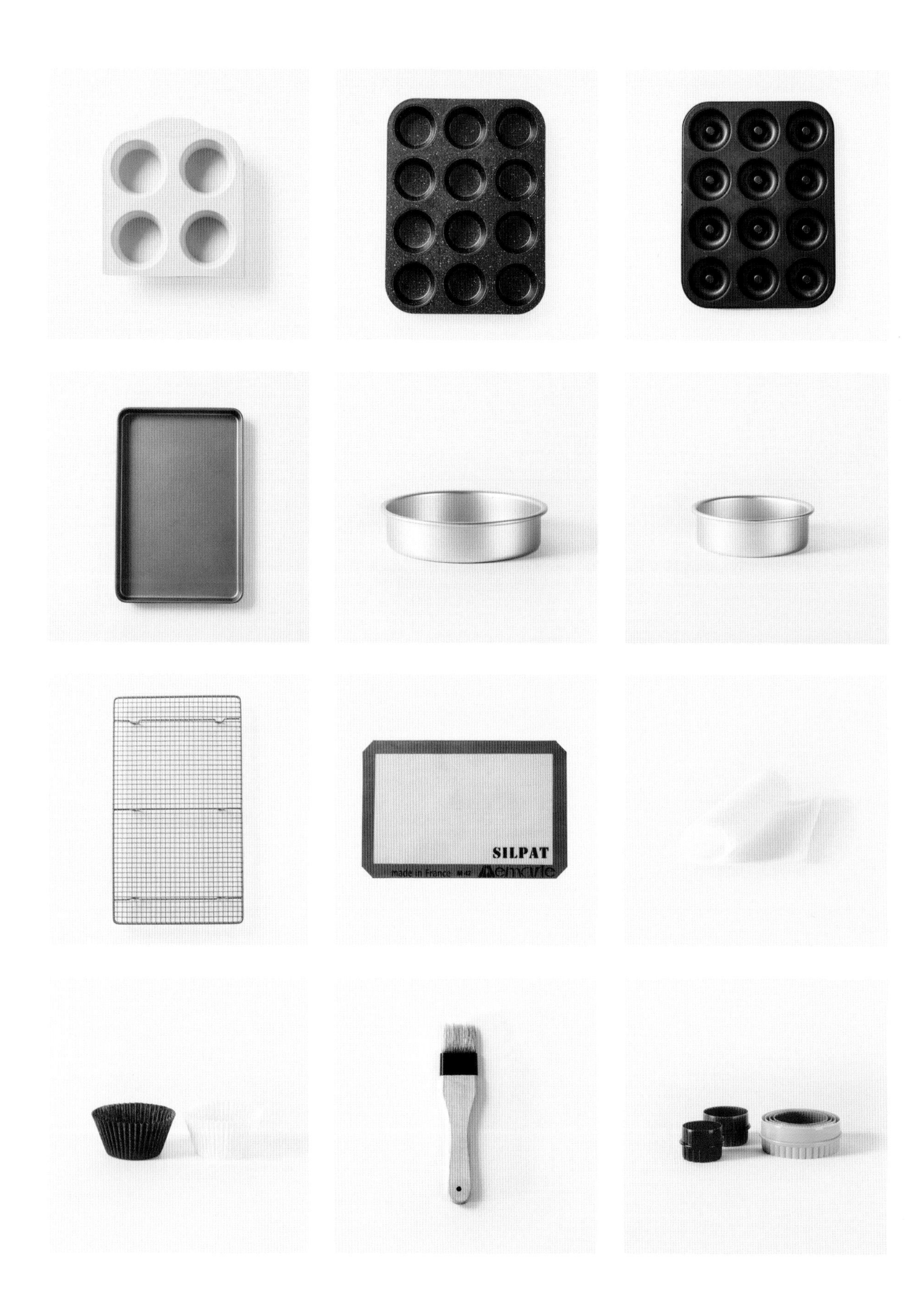
SILPAT
made in France

BAKING TINS, TRAYS & UTENSILS

- Silicone cupcake tray
- Cupcake tin: Wiltshire Easy-Bake Muffin Tray 12-cup Grey, 5.5 cm (2¼ in) bottom × 3 cm (1¼ in) height × 7 cm (2¾ in) top
- Doughnut tin: Wiltshire 12-Hole Doughnut Tin, 7.5 cm (3 in) in diameter × 2.5 cm (1 in) deep
- Baking tray: Wiltshire baking tray, 37 cm (14½ in) × 26 cm (10 in) × 3 cm (1¼ in). I use these for my macarons. You want a flat baking tray for macarons. Don't use old, warped baking trays. And guys, keep them super clean. I find the best way to clean them is by soaking them in some water for a couple of hours, then washing them using a sponge with warm water and soap. They'll look brand new and stay in good condition if you do that every time you use them.
- Large round cake tin: 20 cm (8 in) in diameter, 5 cm (2 in) deep
- Small round cake tin: 15 cm (6 in) in diameter, 5 cm (2 in) deep
- Cooling rack: 43.5 cm (17 in) × 26 cm (10 in) wide, 3 cm (1¼ in) deep
- Silicone baking mats: Silpat non-stick silicone baking mat
- Baking paper: Any brand is fine as long as you don't confuse it with greaseproof paper.
- Cupcake cases: Confetta, 5 cm (2 in) bottom × 4 cm (1½ in) height × 7.5 cm (3 in) top
- Pastry brush
- Cookie cutters

CAKE DECORATING

- Cake turntable: 30 cm (12 in) Iron Cake Turntable. I call it a cake spinny thingy. This is what I use when I frost my cakes. If you get a good heavy iron one, they will last a lifetime and they don't wobble as you spin them.
- Cake leveller: I use a cake leveller to get nice, even layers of cake so that when you frost it, everything looks neat and, when you cut into it, it looks nice and evenly layered. I think it's very important what the inside of your cake looks like.
- Serrated knife: You can also use a serrated knife to trim your cakes instead of a cake leveller.
- Grip mat: AKA grippy thingies. I use these underneath my cake board to help stop it from slipping around on the turntable as I spin it to frost my cakes.
- Cake boards: I use a 20 cm (8 in) foil-lined cardboard cake board. The ones I use are a couple of millimetres thick, but for tall or heavy cakes, you want to use a cake board that is ½ cm (¼ in) thick so that it doesn't warp your cake as you transfer it between the turntable and the fridge.
- Cake scraper: 12 cm (4¾ in) long
- Squeeze bottle: 475 ml (16 fl oz)

CAMERA

I get asked a lot how I photograph and edit my videos and photos. I use a Canon 80D DSLR body and a Canon 50mm F/1.2 lens to shoot all of my videos and photos. You don't need to have super-expensive cameras to photograph food; it's all about practice. I've never read anything about photography or studied it. I just picked up our family camera when I first started and experimented. If you are buying a camera, or you're updating an old camera, BEWARE! Buying cameras online can be very risky! The ones sold online are often grey-market units and the warranty is a bit dodgy. Buy them from a store. They're not nearly as cheap, but, if you're in Australia, you get a 2-year warranty on any Canon product and, if anything goes wrong with the camera in that time, it's much, much easier to get it fixed if you purchased it from a physical store than dealing with people online. Second-hand cameras can be a great way to get a camera if you're on a budget, but do your research.

The program I use to edit my videos is called Final Cut Pro. A free alternative is iMovie, which comes with MacOS. The program I use to edit my photos is Adobe Photoshop. I use a program on my iPad Pro called Adobe Photoshop Sketch to sketch my cupcakes and hand-draw all the titles you see in my videos.

- **Camera:** Canon 80D DSLR camera
- **Lens:** Canon 50mm F/1.2 lens

HEADPHONES

I honestly have the best job ever. I walk around my kitchen all day, baking on my own, with music and YouTube keeping me company. In fact, music inspires a lot of the things I make on The Scran Line. Throughout the book, you will see references to the music that inspired many of my recipes.

KNICK KNACKS

- Large metal whisk
- Sugar thermometer: Digital or regular will work, max temp 200°C (400°F).
- Kitchen blowtorch
- Large and small sieves: I use a large sieve mostly for sifting the combined icing (confectioners') sugar and almond flour. I use the smaller sieves for more delicate work, for example when I want to sprinkle something evenly on cupcakes and macarons.
- Apple corer: To help you core the centre of cupcakes.
- Brushes: I use these for decorating some cakes and cupcakes.
- Small saucepan: For syrups etc.
- Ruler
- Fondant rolling pin

REBEL BASICS

Let's begin with the basics. This chapter is a collection of all my base recipes – my cakes, cupcakes, frostings and sauces.

You'll come back to this chapter a lot since each recipe in the book is an adaptation of these base recipes. For example, the Vanilla cupcakes (page 34) form the basis of a lot of my cupcake designs because they can be coloured and flavoured in a million different ways. The same principle applies for the other recipes in this chapter – I've included them here so that this book isn't 8 million pages long. Ha!

Happy baking!

EASY

MAKES 20 CUPCAKES

20 white cupcake cases

CUPCAKES

- 400 g (14 oz/2⅔ cups) plain (all-purpose) flour
- 320 g (11½ oz) caster (superfine) sugar
- 2 tablespoons unsweetened (Dutch) cocoa powder
- 2 teaspoons baking powder
- 1 teaspoon bicarbonate of soda (baking soda)
- ½ teaspoon fine salt
- 3 eggs
- 190 ml (6½ fl oz) vegetable oil
- 300 ml (10 fl oz) buttermilk
- 2 teaspoons vanilla extract
- 50 ml (1¾ fl oz) red liquid food dye

FROSTING

- 2 batches Cream cheese frosting (page 47)

'Nicki, red velvet cupcakes are the queen of the kitchen' is what Maggie (ex-boss and cupcake fairy godmother; see page 222) said to me very early on in my training with her. 'Make sure they rise and bake perfectly, so they look perfect when people buy them.' Attention to detail was something I became obsessed with back when I worked in a cupcake bakery, and I still apply it to everything I do. It's true though, red velvets are the queens of 'cupcakedom'. They taste amazing, they look gorgeous and they're simple to make. And, when baked the way Maggie taught me, they melt in your mouth and nothing else matters except for when you're going to take the next bite.

Preheat a fan-forced oven to 140°C (275°F) or a conventional oven to 160°C (320°F). Line two cupcake tins with the cupcake cases.

Add the flour, sugar, cocoa powder, baking powder, bicarbonate of soda and salt to a large mixing bowl. Mix on low speed with a hand mixer until combined.

Next, add the eggs, oil, buttermilk, vanilla and red food dye and continue mixing on low speed until everything is well combined. Scrape down the bowl and mix for a final 20 seconds on low speed.

Scoop the batter into your cupcake cases, filling them about halfway. Using an ice-cream scoop to transfer the batter to the cupcake cases makes this a quick and easy process and ensures each case contains exactly the same amount of batter so that the cupcakes bake evenly.

Bake for 40 minutes, or until a toothpick inserted in a cupcake comes out clean. The cupcakes will look shiny and moist on top when they're ready. If they bounce and don't sink when you touch them, they're done. Take care not to overbake these cupcakes because they can dry out quickly, and red velvet cupcakes should be moist and delicate. Once baked, set them aside on a wire rack to cool completely before frosting.

Fit the end of a piping bag with a Wilton 1M tip (see page 13), fill the bag with cream cheese frosting and frost your cupcakes in a signature swirl (see page 14).

VANILLA *cupcakes*

EASY

MAKES **20** CUPCAKES

20 white cupcake cases

CUPCAKES

430g (15 oz) plain (all-purpose) flour
265 g (9½ oz) caster (superfine) sugar
3 teaspoons baking powder
½ teaspoon fine salt
125 g (4½ oz/½ cup) unsalted butter, softened
2 large eggs
375 ml (12½ fl oz/1½ cups) full-cream (whole) milk
125 ml (4 fl oz/½ cup) vegetable oil
2 tablespoons Greek yoghurt (or sour cream)
1 teaspoon vanilla extract or vanilla bean paste

FROSTING

2 batches American buttercream frosting (page 45) or Swiss meringue buttercream frosting (page 46)

'Hey Nick, why don't you cream the butter and sugar together?'

I'm glad you asked. This is literally the most common question I get about this recipe, so let me answer it now ... But not before I tell you that these vanilla cupcakes are super moist, slightly denser than regular cupcakes, and they taste amazing. And! The recipe is super versatile; you can pretty much flavour it with anything and colour it with any colour that you want (as you're about to discover in this book ...).

Now, down to business. Most vanilla cupcake recipes have you cream the butter and sugar together, which is called the 'creaming method'. Instead, I use the reverse-creaming method, which is when the butter goes in with the dry ingredients and is mixed until it resembles fine crumbs. There are a couple of reasons for this: firstly, I used to work in a bakery and, in a bakery, you'll find any way you can to save time. The reverse-creaming method is much quicker than the creaming method. Secondly, I use this method because it yields a much moister cake. The creaming method, although the batter comes out a little fluffier, usually makes a drier mixture. Lastly, I use this method because there is less chance of overmixing the batter than with the creaming method.

Preheat a fan-forced oven to 140°C (275°F) or a conventional oven to 160°C (320°F). Line two cupcake tins with the cupcake cases.

Add the flour, sugar, baking powder and salt to a large mixing bowl and mix with a hand mixer until well combined.

Next, add the softened butter and mix on low speed until the mixture reaches a crumbly, sand-like texture.

Add the eggs, milk, oil, yoghurt and vanilla, and mix on low speed until all the dry ingredients are incorporated. Scrape down the side of the bowl and mix for a final 20 seconds. It's at this point that you can add any flavourings or food-gel colourings to the batter.

Fill each case three-quarters of the way. Using an ice-cream scoop to transfer the batter to the cupcake cases makes this a quick and easy process and ensures each case contains exactly the same amount of batter so that the cupcakes bake evenly. Bake for 40–50 minutes, or until a toothpick inserted in the middle of a cupcake comes out clean. Allow the cupcakes to cool completely on a wire rack before frosting.

Fit the end of a piping bag with a Wilton 1M tip (see page 13), fill your bag with frosting and frost your cupcakes in a signature swirl (see page 14).

VANILLA cake

EASY

MAKES **1 BATCH** CAKE BATTER / SERVES **15**

CAKE

430 g (15 oz) plain (all-purpose) flour
265 g (9½ oz) caster (superfine) sugar
3 teaspoons baking powder
½ teaspoon fine salt
125 g (4½ oz/½ cup) unsalted butter, softened
2 large eggs
375 ml (12½ fl oz/1½ cups) full-cream (whole) milk
125 ml (4 fl oz/½ cup) vegetable oil
2 tablespoons Greek yoghurt (or sour cream)
1 teaspoon vanilla extract or vanilla bean paste

FROSTING

2 batches Swiss meringue buttercream frosting (page 46)

Please note: To make the six-layered cake as shown in the image, you'll need to make two batches of vanilla cake batter. Two batches of Swiss meringue frosting are enough to cover this six-layered cake.

My vanilla cake recipe is just delicious! It's moist and slightly dense, which is what you want in a cake. Fluffy cakes aren't meant to be decorated like the ones you'll see in this book. The best part about this recipe is that it's so moist that you don't need to add any simple syrup (sugar syrup) to keep it from drying out. Same deal with the cupcakes, and you can add any flavourings or colours you like to this recipe: berries, liqueurs, food-gel colouring – the options are endless!

Preheat a fan-forced oven to 140°C (275°F) or a conventional oven to 160°C (320°F). Spray three 20 cm (8 in) cake tins with oil spray and line the bottoms with baking paper (see page 10). Set aside.

Add the flour, sugar, baking powder and salt to a large mixing bowl and mix with a hand mixer until well combined.

Next, add the softened butter and mix on low speed until the mixture reaches a crumbly, sand-like texture.

Add the eggs, milk, oil, yoghurt and vanilla, and mix on low speed until all the dry ingredients are incorporated. Scrape down the side of the bowl and mix for another 20 seconds. It's at this point that you can add any additional flavourings or food-gel colourings to the batter.

Divide the cake mixture between the three tins. I find that using an ice-cream scoop makes it easy to distribute the batter evenly, ensuring that all three cakes bake at the same rate.

Bake for 50–60 minutes, or until a toothpick inserted in the middle of a cake comes out clean. If the toothpick is coated in wet batter, continue baking, for 10 minutes at a time, until fully baked.

Allow the cakes to cool to room temperature in the tins, then chill them in the fridge overnight, still in their tins (you can wrap the tins in plastic wrap if you like). Chilling your cakes overnight makes them easier to trim and decorate, so I always bake my cakes the day before I decorate them. You can bake the cakes up to a week in advance and freeze them by tightly wrapping them in plastic wrap. To thaw the cakes, take them out the night before decorating.

To trim, fill and crumb-coat your cake, see page 10.

To frost your cake, see page 12.

CHOCOLATE *cupcakes*

EASY

MAKES 10 CUPCAKES

10 brown cupcake cases

CUPCAKES

175 g (6 oz) plain (all-purpose) flour
225 g (8 oz) caster (superfine) sugar
50 g (1¾ oz) unsweetened (Dutch) cocoa powder
½ teaspoon bicarbonate of soda (baking soda)
½ teaspoon fine salt
175 g (6 oz) unsalted butter, softened
2 large eggs, at room temperature
175 ml (6 fl oz) full-cream (whole) milk

FROSTING

1 batch chocolate-flavoured American buttercream frosting (page 45) or chocolate-flavoured Swiss meringue buttercream frosting (page 46)

I kind of have a love-hate relationship with chocolate. We're seeing a therapist at the moment; she just needs to sort out her boundaries. Sometimes I hate chocolate. Not the taste. I get mad with chocolate because it gets everywhere when I film with it – on the floor, my hands, my feet, the bench. It gets on every bowl in the kitchen. I get mad at it and stay away from it for a couple of days but, when I do use it, my fave way to eat chocolate is in the form of this cupcake, especially when it has just come out of the oven. OMG yum! It's really moist, and has a slightly dense brownie-like texture, yet it's still 'cakey', which makes it perfect for cupcakes and cakes.

Preheat a fan-forced oven to 140°C (275°F) or a conventional oven to 160°C (320°F). Line a cupcake tin with the cupcake cases.

Add the flour, sugar, cocoa powder, bicarbonate of soda and salt to a large mixing bowl. Mix on low speed with a hand mixer until combined.

Next, add the softened butter and continue mixing on low speed until the mixture reaches a crumbly, sand-like texture.

Add the eggs and milk and mix again on low speed until all the dry ingredients are incorporated. Scrape down the side of the bowl and mix for a final 20 seconds.

Fill each case three-quarters of the way. Using an ice-cream scoop to transfer the batter to the cupcake cases makes this a quick and easy process and ensures each case contains exactly the same amount of batter so that the cupcakes bake evenly. Bake for 40–50 minutes, or until a toothpick inserted in the centre of a cupcake comes out clean. Allow the cupcakes to cool completely on a wire rack before frosting.

Fit the end of a piping bag with a Wilton 1M tip (see page 13), fill the bag with frosting and frost your cupcakes in a signature swirl (see page 14).

CHOCOLATE *cake*

EASY

MAKES **1 BATCH** CAKE BATTER / SERVES **15**

My chocolate cake recipe is just like my cupcake recipe, but I wanted to include it for you guys so that you can understand the basics of how to bake and construct it. You can pretty much add anything to this cake, such as berries, alcohol (to taste) or chopped nuts, to put your own twist on it.

CAKE

350 g (12½ oz/2⅓ cups) plain (all-purpose) flour
450 g (1 lb) caster (superfine) sugar
100 g (3½ oz) unsweetened (Dutch) cocoa powder
1 teaspoon bicarbonate of soda (baking soda)
1 teaspoon fine salt
350 g (12½ oz) unsalted butter, softened
4 large eggs, at room temperature
350 ml (12 fl oz) full-cream (whole) milk

FROSTING

2 batches chocolate-flavoured Swiss meringue buttercream frosting (page 46)

Please note: To make the six-layered cake as shown in the image, you'll need to make two batches of chocolate cake batter. Two batches of Swiss meringue frosting are enough to cover this six-layered cake.

Preheat a fan-forced oven to 140°C (275°F) or a conventional oven to 160°C (320°F). Spray three 20 cm (8 in) cake tins with oil spray and line the bottoms with baking paper (see page 10). Set aside.

Add the flour, sugar, cocoa powder, bicarbonate of soda and salt to a large mixing bowl and mix with a hand mixer until well combined.

Next, add the softened butter and mix on low speed until the batter reaches a crumbly, sand-like texture.

Add the eggs and milk and mix again on low speed until all the dry ingredients are incorporated. Scrape down the side of the bowl and mix for another 20 seconds. It's at this point that you can add any additional flavourings or food-gel colourings to the batter.

Divide the cake mixture between the three tins. I find that using an ice-cream scoop makes it easy to distribute the batter evenly, ensuring that all three cakes bake at the same rate.

Bake for 50–60 minutes, or until a toothpick inserted in the middle of the cake comes out clean. If the toothpick is coated with wet batter, continue baking, for 10 minutes at a time, until fully baked.

Allow the cakes to cool to room temperature in the tins, then chill them in the fridge overnight, still in their tins (you can wrap the tins in plastic wrap if you like). Chilling your cakes overnight makes them easier to trim and decorate, so I always bake my cakes the day before I decorate them. You can bake the cakes up to a week in advance and freeze them by tightly wrapping them in plastic wrap. To thaw the cakes, take them out the night before decorating.

To trim, fill and crumb-coat your cake, see page 10.

To frost your cake, see page 12.

MEDIUM

MAKES **30** SANDWICHED MACARONS

150 g (5½ oz) almond flour (see page 18)
150 g (5½ oz) icing (confectioners') sugar
110 g (4 oz) liquefied egg whites (see page 18)
150 g (5½ oz) granulated sugar
37 g (1¼ oz) water (yes, grams!)
1 teaspoon vanilla extract or vanilla bean paste

Note: Guys, for all my macaron recipes, I've asked that the ingredients are given in weight measurements only. This is because you must weigh everything out precisely to get great, consistent results. Check out Macaron troubleshooting (page 19) for the most common problems.

If you've ever felt defeated by this little French cookie, this recipe will make it feel less intimidating for you.

There are two ways to make the meringue for macarons: the French meringue method, where you simply add the sugar to the egg whites, or the Italian meringue method, where you make a hot sugar syrup and add it to the egg whites. I prefer the Italian method, as I find it yields much more consistent results.

I recommend that you measure everything out *before* you start this recipe, because everything moves quickly when making macarons and you won't have time to stop and measure things once you've started. After a couple of goes it'll feel as easy as making cupcakes. It's really not that difficult, promise!

Line two baking trays with silicone baking mats or baking paper (not greaseproof paper). If you're using baking paper, you can dab the baking trays with a little of the macaron batter once you've made it. This will help the paper stick so that it doesn't fly around in the oven and ruins your macarons.

Combine the almond flour and icing sugar in a food processor and pulse 4–5 times, or until well combined. (Take care not to pulse too much, otherwise you'll risk releasing the oils in the almonds.) Pulsing these ingredients does two things: it helps to get rid of any lumps in the sugar and helps to grind the almond flour to a finer consistency. Once you have pulsed the ingredients, sift them once through a fine-mesh sieve. Alternatively, you can sift the two ingredients together without first pulsing in a food processor, but make sure to sift them at least three times.

Transfer the almond mixture to a large, clean glass or metal mixing bowl. Add half the liquefied egg whites and use a spatula to mix everything together until the mixture forms a paste. Cover with plastic wrap and set aside at room temperature.

To make the sugar syrup, combine the granulated sugar and water in a small saucepan. Give it a gentle stir with a teaspoon to make sure they're well combined. After this point, don't mix the syrup again. Bring to the boil over a medium–high heat, then reduce the heat a little and simmer. As the syrup bubbles away, it will splatter small bubbles of sugared water on the side of the pan. Use a pastry brush dipped in a little water to brush the bubbles back into the syrup. This will help prevent the syrup from crystallising.

For this recipe, you'll need a sugar thermometer to help you measure the temperature of the syrup. When the syrup reaches 115°C (239°F), add the remaining egg whites to the bowl of a stand mixer fitted with the whisk attachment and whisk on a medium–high speed to help break them apart and get them frothy.

When the syrup reaches 118°C (244°F), carefully pour the hot syrup into the egg whites in a slow and steady stream. Start by whisking on a medium speed for 1 minute, then increase the speed to high and whisk until the egg whites become frothy. Please be careful when doing this part, firstly because the syrup is hot, but also because if you add your syrup too quickly, you'll cook the egg whites and they'll turn to soup. Once you've poured all the sugar

CONTINUED ON PAGE 44

syrup into the egg whites, continue whisking on high speed for about 3 minutes before adding the vanilla extract. It's at this point that you can also add any food-gel colouring or food flavourings to the meringue.

Continue whisking on high speed for another 4–5 minutes. Once the meringue has become thick and glossy and has cooled down almost to room temperature, stop the mixer and gently scrape down the bowl, then whisk on high speed for another couple of minutes.

The next part is the mixing stage, otherwise known as 'macaronage', and is super important. It's where most people go wrong – including me, until I took a trip to Paris and was physically shown how to do it by a French pastry chef.

Grab a spatula full of the meringue and fold it into the almond-sugar mixture until well combined. This allows the mixture to thin out a little before you add the rest of the meringue. Different people mix macaron batter in different ways; some count the number of times they mix, but I think it's better to know what consistency to look out for. I like to go around the bowl with my spatula and then through the middle. You want to continue doing that until you reach the 'ribbon stage' (see page 18). That's when you know the batter is ready to pipe.

Spoon the batter into a piping bag fitted with a medium round tip. Pipe 60 rounds of batter, about 3 cm (1¼ in) in diameter, on the prepared trays, being sure to space them 2 cm (¾ in) apart. Gently tap the tray on your work surface. This will help remove any air bubbles that might be lurking in your batter. It's at this stage that you can add any small sprinkles or freeze-dried berries on top.

The next thing you want to do is let your macarons dry out in the open air for about 30 minutes to 1 hour (the drying time depends on the weather, or how much humidity is in the air). Drying your macarons helps them to form a skin. The skin is super important because it means that when you bake your macarons and the steam escapes from the shells, it will escape from the bottom, not the top, forming the iconic 'feet' on your macarons. So, when you can gently prod your uncooked macarons and they're not sticky to the touch, you know they're ready to bake. Ten minutes before the end of the drying time, preheat a fan-forced oven to 140°C (275°F) or a conventional oven to 160°C (320°F).

Place each tray of macarons, one at a time, in the centre of the oven and bake for 12 minutes. If you feel your oven is causing the macarons to brown on one side (usually the side closest to the fan), turn the tray around about halfway through. Once they're baked, let them cool completely before you try to remove them from the tray.

To finish your macarons, you can fill them with any number of fillings: lemon curd, chocolate ganache, buttercream or different frostings; the filling options are endless. For a plain vanilla macaron, I'd recommend Swiss meringue buttercream frosting (page 46) or Chocolate ganache frosting (page 49).

AMERICAN BUTTERCREAM *frosting*

EASY

MAKES **1 BATCH** FROSTING

- 500 g (1 lb 2 oz/2 cups) unsalted butter, softened
- 500 g (1 lb 2 oz/4 cups) icing (confectioners') sugar
- 2–4 teaspoons vanilla extract or vanilla bean paste
- 2 tablespoons full-cream (whole) milk (at room temperature); optional, but recommended

Notes

For chocolate-flavoured buttercream, add 80 g (2¾ oz) sifted unsweetened (Dutch) cocoa powder with the icing sugar.

My cake recipes often call for more than one batch of frosting. Depending on the size of your mixing bowl, you may need to split the frosting into two batches when flavouring and colouring it.

Butter and sugar. Two magic ingredients in the baking world that, when combined, form a perfectly smooth and pipeable magic substance called frosting that you can pile on top of your cupcakes and cakes, or pipe into your macarons. Don't skimp on the vanilla, guys – the more the better! But don't bother adding it if you're making chocolate buttercream (see the Notes) – you won't taste it at all.

Add your softened butter to the bowl of a stand mixer fitted with the paddle attachment. You can also use a hand mixer for this recipe, but if you do use a hand mixer, make sure your bowl is large. Mix the butter on low speed to begin with, then switch to the highest speed and mix for 5 minutes until the butter is fluffy and turns pale in colour.

Stop your mixer and scrape down the side of the bowl using a spatula. Add the icing sugar and vanilla extract and mix again on low speed. LOW SPEED, PEOPLE! The last thing you need is to end up in a sugar dust storm!

Once all the sugar has been incorporated, it's safe to turn your mixer up to high speed. Continue beating on high speed for about 5–6 minutes, or until the butter turns pale in colour and becomes fluffy again. If you want to soften your buttercream and make it a little smoother, add the milk and continue mixing for another couple of minutes on medium speed. At this stage, you can also add any food flavourings or food-gel colourings.

SWISS MERINGUE BUTTERCREAM *frosting*

MEDIUM

MAKES **1 BATCH** FROSTING

- 200 g (7 oz) fresh egg whites (usually about 6 large eggs)
- 200 g (7 oz) granulated sugar
- 500 g (1 lb 2 oz/2 cups) unsalted butter, softened
- 1 teaspoon vanilla extract or vanilla bean paste

Notes

To make chocolate-flavoured buttercream, add 40 g (1½ oz) sifted unsweetened (Dutch) cocoa powder when you add the vanilla extract.

My cake recipes often call for more than one batch of frosting. Depending on the size of your mixing bowl, you may need to split the frosting into two batches when flavouring and colouring it.

OK, this frosting is in direct response to all the people who message me asking for frosting that isn't too sweet or grainy. If that's what you're after, then this frosting is for you! This frosting looks silky, which makes it perfect for frosting smooth cakes. Be careful though, because it can be a little softer than the firmer American buttercream frosting (page 45). So, if it's a warm day, I'd use American buttercream frosting instead.

Begin by filling a large saucepan one-quarter of the way with water. Let it come to a gentle boil over a medium–high heat.

Separate your egg whites from your yolks in a large, very clean, glass or metal mixing bowl. We only need the egg whites for this recipe, so you can store the yolks in an airtight container in the fridge to use for something else. (My go-to recipe for using up egg yolks is custard. Yum!) Add your sugar to the egg whites and use a hand whisk to mix them together.

Place your bowl on top of the pan of boiling water, making sure the bottom of the bowl doesn't touch the water. This is called the double-boiler method and is a very gentle way of cooking or melting something.

Gently whisk your egg white and sugar mixture for about 3–4 minutes, or until the sugar is completely dissolved. Check that it's dissolved by running it through two fingers. If you can't feel the sugar granules, then it's time to take it off the heat. If you can, then continue whisking for another 2–3 minutes and keep testing until you can no longer feel any granules.

Transfer the mixture to the bowl of a stand mixer fitted with the whisk attachment and whisk on high speed for about 4–5 minutes. The mixture will become thick and glossy and will begin to cool.

Gradually add the softened butter, 1 tablespoon at a time, while the mixer is on high speed. At first, your egg whites will deflate and look like the butter is causing them to split, but don't panic! It will come back together. It takes a couple of minutes for the butter and meringue to become best friends.

Once you have added all the butter, add the vanilla extract and mix first on low speed to combine, then on high speed for 5 minutes.

You'll know it's done when the frosting has come together, has turned pale in colour (if you're making vanilla) and is nice and fluffy.

If you find your frosting is too aerated, then mix at the lowest speed for about 10 minutes and it will become perfectly smooth again.

CREAM CHEESE *frosting*

MEDIUM

MAKES **1 BATCH** FROSTING

250 g (9 oz/1 cup) full-fat cream cheese blocks (not spreadable), chilled
250 g (9 oz/1 cup) unsalted butter, softened
350 g (12½ oz) icing (confectioners') sugar
150 g (5½ oz/1½ cups) powdered milk (skim or full-fat)
2 teaspoons vanilla extract or vanilla bean paste

Notes

It's important to always mix this frosting on high speed. The only time you mix it on low speed is after you've added the dry ingredients. Mixing on high speed helps to aerate the frosting, giving it volume and making it easier to pipe.

For chocolate-flavoured frosting, add 40 g (1½ oz) sifted unsweetened (Dutch) cocoa powder with the icing sugar.

Guys, this is hands down my favourite frosting. The best thing about it is that it's not as sweet as you'd think because the slight tanginess from the cream cheese helps to cut through the sweetness. It is my fave frosting because it just tastes amazing, and the addition of powdered milk makes it extra creamy!

Place the cream cheese and butter in the bowl of a stand mixer fitted with the paddle attachment. Alternatively, you can use a hand mixer. Mix on low speed to begin with, to help break up the cream cheese a little, then increase the speed to high for a couple of minutes to help combine the cream cheese and butter.

After a couple of minutes, stop your mixer and scrape down the side of the bowl with a spatula. Add the icing sugar, powdered milk and vanilla. Mix on low speed until the dry ingredients are fully incorporated, then bring the speed back up to high. Continue beating on high speed until your frosting is fluffy and turns pale in colour.

VEGAN BUTTERCREAM *frosting*

EASY

MAKES 1 BATCH FROSTING

125 g (4½ oz/½ cup) butter-flavoured Crisco shortening, at room temperature
300 g (10½ oz) dairy-free/vegan margarine, chilled
500 g (1 lb 2 oz/4 cups) icing (confectioners') sugar
3 teaspoons vanilla extract or vanilla bean paste
2 tablespoons plant-based milk (I use almond milk); optional, but recommended

Notes

For chocolate-flavoured vegan buttercream, add 80 g (2¾ oz) sifted unsweetened (Dutch) cocoa powder with the icing sugar.

My cake recipes often call for more than one batch of frosting. Depending on the size of your mixing bowl, you may need to split the frosting into two batches when flavouring and colouring it.

This frosting is for my lovely, very vocal vegan followers! I hear you. Here's my vegan vanilla buttercream frosting, which can be flavoured with chocolate too. It's smooth, delicious and can be used for cakes or cupcakes.

Add your shortening and margarine to the bowl of a stand mixer fitted with the paddle attachment. You can also use a hand mixer for this recipe, but if you do use a hand mixer, make sure your bowl is large. Mix on low speed to begin with, to allow everything to combine, then increase the speed to high. Mix on high speed for 5 minutes, or until the mixture is fluffy and turns pale in colour.

Stop your mixer and scrape down the side of the bowl using a spatula. Add the icing sugar and vanilla, and mix on low speed.

Once all the dry ingredients are incorporated, it's safe to turn your mixer up to high speed. Beat for about 5–6 minutes, or until the mixture turns pale in colour and becomes fluffy again. If you want to soften your buttercream and make it a little smoother, add the milk and continue mixing for another couple of minutes on a medium speed. It's also at this stage that you can add any food flavourings or food-gel colourings.

CHOCOLATE GANACHE *frosting*

EASY

MAKES **1 BATCH** FROSTING

700 g (1 lb 9 oz) dark or milk chocolate buttons
100 g (3½ oz) unsalted butter
250 ml (8½ fl oz/1 cup) thick (double/heavy) cream

Note

My cake recipes often call for more than one batch of frosting. Depending on the size of your mixing bowl, you may need to split the frosting into two batches when flavouring it.

The thing about chocolate ganache frosting is that if you have no self-control, it becomes very dangerous. Because even in its warm, melted state, you'll want to drink it. You can use my chocolate ganache frosting in two ways: unwhipped or whipped. Whipped is almost like eating a very rich, fluffy mousse, and unwhipped is nice and dense – perfect for filling cakes.

Combine the chocolate, butter and cream in a large, microwave-safe bowl. Microwave on high, for 20 seconds at a time, mixing between each interval until smooth. Once fully melted, cover with plastic wrap and leave to set. Alternatively, you can use the double-boiler method. Fill a large saucepan one-third of the way with water and bring to the boil. Place the chocolate, butter and cream in a large glass or metal mixing bowl and set it over the pan, making sure the bottom of the bowl doesn't touch the water. Gently stir the mixture until it is completely melted and smooth. Remove from the heat and leave to set at room temperature.

To soften the ganache to spreading or piping consistency, microwave on high for 10 seconds at a time, mixing well between each interval, until it becomes soft enough to spread easily but firm enough to hold its shape. If you soften it too much, don't panic, just let it sit at room temperate again until it firms up enough to use.

To use it in its whipped state after it has set, add it to the bowl of a stand mixer fitted with the paddle attachment and start by whipping on low speed. Once it has softened a little and looks slightly paler, turn the mixer up to high and whip for 5–6 minutes until it becomes light, fluffy and pale in colour.

SALTED CARAMEL *sauce*

EASY

MAKES **375 ML (12½ FL OZ/ 1½ CUPS)**

330 g (11½ oz/1½ cups) granulated sugar
2 tablespoons glucose syrup (or corn syrup); see Tip below
250 ml (8½ fl oz/1 cup) thick (double/ heavy) cream, warmed
50 g (1¾ oz) unsalted butter
1 teaspoon sea salt flakes

Tip

Before you measure your glucose syrup, spray your measuring spoon with some oil to make it easy for the syrup to slide off the spoon.

If you've never tried salted caramel, you're missing out. The first time I heard about it I thought: that's gross. Caramel is supposed to be sweet. But the saltiness in this recipe helps cut through the sweetness and makes it even tastier. It's really easy to make, but if you're a mini baker, you'll definitely need to get an adult to help you out.

To make the caramel, place the sugar, glucose syrup and 125 ml (4 fl oz/½ cup) water in a large saucepan set over a medium–low heat. Bring to the boil and cook for 10–12 minutes until it becomes a deep gold colour, but not dark brown. DO NOT STIR at any point, otherwise you risk crystallising your syrup. When the caramel begins to colour, it will darken quickly so keep a close eye on it. Also keep in mind that it will continue cooking once it's off the heat, so work quickly.

Remove the syrup from the heat once it reaches the correct colour. Slowly add the warmed cream. Use a wooden spoon to slowly mix the cream into the hot syrup. It will bubble and splatter. Be very careful. Next, add the butter and salt and whisk to combine. Allow to cool completely before using.

This sauce can be stored in an airtight container for up to 2 weeks in the fridge.

EASY

MAKES **625 ML (21 FL OZ/ 2½ CUPS)**

- 100 g (3½ oz) good-quality dark chocolate buttons
- 250 g (9 oz/1 cup) unsalted butter
- 250 g (9 oz) brown sugar
- 75 ml (2½ fl oz) thickened (whipping) cream

Note

If you have any leftover chocolate sauce, you can store it in the fridge, in an airtight container, for 2–3 weeks or freeze it for 4 weeks.

You will literally never find a better or easier chocolate sauce than this one. I'm not even afraid to say that, 'cos it's true. Not only that, but this recipe is super versatile too. You can use it in the centre of cupcakes, drizzle it over cakes or even drizzle it on ice cream while you sit on the couch watching your fave movie with your dog looking at you with puppy-dog eyes 'cos he wants some, but dogs can't have chocolate. They just can't. I know it doesn't make sense, but it's a cruel world.

Wow, that got dark ... Here's my chocolate sauce recipe!

Add all the ingredients to a large, microwave-safe bowl and microwave on high, for 20 seconds at a time, mixing well between each interval until smooth.

To thin out your sauce for things like drizzling on cupcakes and cakes, simply microwave for 10 seconds at a time, stirring between each interval until it's thin enough to drizzle.

HEY NICK,

I get loads of emails and questions in the comments section of my posts, and I do my best to answer as many of them as I can. Here's a list of the most common questions you guys ask and some funny ones that I wanted to include for a laugh.

You can always ask me questions through my website, www.thescranline.com, or on social media :)

NICK QUESTIONS

(That's right: I refer to myself in the third person.)

Do you eat all your creations?

If, by 'eat', you mean every single crumb, then no. Do I taste them? Yes, I taste most of what I make to make sure it's good to go, but I've been making cupcakes every single day for six years and I know how everything will taste.

How much of your week do you dedicate to baking?

I bake every day.

Do you plan to start a bakery of your own one day? And, if so, where would it be?

Maybe. I'm not really sure. I have a very clear idea in my head of what it would look like, but I'm not sure where it would be or if I would even do it. I loved working in a bakery and I miss it some days. I think it would be a lot of hard work to return to it, but a lot of fun! And I know you guys want it to happen.

What's your fave thing you've made?

So, this is like asking me to answer who is my favourite child. I don't have children, but I love everything I've made. A few of my designs stick out to me though. My Bubblepop electric cupcakes (page 56), Mint choc chip freakshake cupcakes (page 130) and my Diamond heart cupcakes (page 172) are a few of my faves.

Where do you find inspiration for all of your crazy-interesting flavours?

Pop culture! Design, architecture, songs, artists, colours, shapes, etc. Lots and lots of different places. Like most people, I go through phases. Right now, I'm going through a *Drag Race* phase. I'm super inspired by *Drag Race*.

What's your favourite flavour?

Of cupcakes? Red velvet with cream cheese frosting. Of macarons? My Tiramisu macarons are to die for – check them out on my website!

How long did it take you to be recognised on a large scale?

So, it's been a slow process. It's taken me about four years to get the number of followers I have on YouTube, Instagram and Facebook.

When was the first time you ever felt like you had 'made it'?

Ha! I've never really felt like I made it. I mean, I still feel weird saying I'm a YouTuber, especially because when you say that to people in Australia, they look at you like you just told them you're an alien from another planet. For me, I've only ever wanted to be as great as the people I look up to. One of the very first cake YouTubers I ever started watching was Elise from My Cupcake Addiction. So, first of all, Elise is amazing! To this day I don't know how she's able to do what she does and raise a family. But! Above all, Elise is such a lovely person and is so generous too.

On my first trip to America, I was on my own in Santa Monica and I happened to be on Twitter and saw Elise tweet out that she was in Santa Monica too, so I tweeted back saying let's hang out and we met up and it was amazing! You know how they say never meet your heroes? That's not true for YouTubers. Every YouTuber I've met has been amazing.

OK, so from that day we became friends. Not long after I'd come back home I was at the gym one day. Before I left for the gym I checked my follower count on Facebook. I finished my workout and, by the time I got back, I had gained 4,000 followers on Facebook. In 40 minutes. I lost my mind trying to figure out what had happened. Then I discovered that Elise has shared one of my videos on her page. That was the moment I felt like I was officially part of the amazing group of YouTubers that I loved and looked up to. Not so much a 'made it' feeling, but an even better feeling of being respected and noticed by someone I really looked up to.

What got you interested in baking and putting it on Instagram?

OK, I'm so glad one of you asked this question because this is the perfect opportunity to tell you about Laura Vitale from Laura In The Kitchen.

The Scran Line began as a blog, but then I discovered YouTube. Back then, there weren't that many people doing food videos – probably about 10. One of them was Laura Vitale, and she's still doing them.

Laura's story inspires me a lot. She grew up in Italy and moved to America with her dad and they started a pizza shop. When the financial crisis happened, they closed the shop and she started making cooking videos with her husband.

I became obsessed. The way she talks about food, the way she presents it, her connection and obvious on-screen enthusiasm for what she makes is what inspired me to start my own channel. Laura Vitale is the reason I made the shift over to YouTube.

Do you sell your cupcakes, cakes and macarons?

Nope, I don't really even identify as a baker. I create online content for my brand. That content happens to be what I'm really passionate about, which is baking. And before anyone asks, no I cannot make you a cake. And before anyone asks (and they have), I cannot ship a cake to Alaska. How do you even expect that to arrive in one piece?! What I love most about my job is seeing that you guys have recreated my recipes. That's what my aim is: to encourage you to get in the kitchen and make these things yourselves.

Have you always wanted to bake or considered other options? I think you would make a good graphic designer, have you ever thought about that?

I am actually a graphic designer. I studied graphic design for three years after I finished high school and worked as a graphic designer for a year before I was fired during the global financial crisis. I didn't go back to it because sitting at a desk all day being forced to be creative didn't work for me.

Do you have kids?

No. I have nephews. It's like having kids, but you don't have to deal with the tantrums and you get to do fun things with them like give them chocolate or play. But kudos to all the parents out there. I'm too selfish with my time right now to have kids. Do I want kids? Yes. I come from a big family and I'd like to have my own kids one day.

My God, I feel like I'm writing a Dear Diary ...

'Dear diary,

Today I met the person I think I'm going to have kids with.'

Next day ...

'Dear Diary, he just smiled at me because he was serving me at the café he works at and smiling at customers is a part of his job.' **Drops ice cream on the diary from the massive tub he is holding because the love affair ended before it even began**

How do you photograph your cupcakes, cakes and macarons, and how do you make your videos?

OK, so this is going to potentially sound a bit sharp-edged and maybe a little rude. But I get asked this one a lot. I don't share my photographing techniques with anyone. I feel my job is to share my knowledge and skills when it comes to baking, but, when it comes to how I create my videos and photos, I don't want to share them because I worked super hard to develop my own style and I don't want to encourage any copycats. There's nothing I hate more than people copying other people's work.

My advice to those who want to learn how to photograph is to either take classes, or you could do what I did and just pick up a camera – any camera will do – and experiment. I learned everything I know by just mucking around with my first camera.

Does music inspire your ideas for your cakes?

Are dogs a man's best friend? Yes! Music inspires pretty much everything I make, especially music by pop divas like Beyoncé, Madonna, Ariana, Nicki, Rhianna, Xtina, RuPaul and, of course, Gaga.

As a future baker, I want to make a YouTube channel. What equipment do you use to do your videos??

Check out the Tools & Equipment section (page 21).

What does The Scran Line mean?

'Scran' is the word the Royal Australian Navy use for food. So, when we'd stand in line for food, we'd stand in the scran line.

Do you believe in ghosts?

I don't want to.

Have you ever dropped a fully finished cake? If yes what did you do with it?

No, but when I first started making cakes, I used to put simple syrup on them, and one day one of my cakes was so moist it just completely collapsed. No more simple syrup for me!

How old were you when you made your first mega cupcake or cake (a really extravagant cake)?

Like, two years ago. I only started making proper multi-layered cakes quite recently. I spent about six months practising and watching a lot of tutorials on YouTube before I made my first cake on The Scran Line.

How are you so motivated?

I'm not always. You guys keep me motivated. Music plays a big part too.

REBEL ALL-STARS

You know how when someone asks a parent who their favourite child is and they say 'I love all my kids equally'?

We all know that's not entirely true ...

I have over 450 kids. Here are my favourites.

BUBBLEPOP ELECTRIC *cupcakes*

HARD

MAKES **20** CUPCAKES

INSPIRED BY: **BUBBLEPOP ELECTRIC – GWEN STEFANI**

20 white cupcake cases

PINK GELATIN BUBBLES

20–25 food-safe water balloons
8 tablespoons cold water
28 g (1 oz) powdered gelatin
1–2 drops deep pink food-gel colouring
1 teaspoon strawberry flavouring

CUPCAKES

1 batch Vanilla cupcakes (page 34)
1 teaspoon bubblegum flavouring (available online)
3 drops deep pink food-gel colouring
185 g (6½ oz/1 cup) assorted pink sprinkles (anything you can find – the more varied, the better)

BUBBLEGUM GOO

250 g (9 oz) Wilton white candy melts
250 ml (8½ fl oz/1 cup) thickened (whipping) cream
1 teaspoon bubblegum or strawberry flavouring
2 drops blue food-gel colouring

FROSTING

1–2 drops blue food-gel colouring
1 teaspoon bubblegum or strawberry flavouring
½ batch American buttercream frosting (page 45)

Iconic. This is the single most iconic cupcake on The Scran line. That's why it's the first main recipe in the book. It's gorgeous.

PINK GELATIN BUBBLES

These are food-safe, but are meant purely for decoration and not for eating – the bubblegum flavouring is in there just to create the smell. I mean, you could try eating them, but you'd be chewing for months and it would be like eating plastic! You'll also need to prepare these a few days before you bake the cake to give them ample time to dry.

Start by blowing up 20–25 food-safe water balloons to about the same size as the width of the cupcakes. Attach each blown-up balloon to a paper straw or cake-pop stick using tape. Spray a paper towel with some oil and lightly coat each balloon. This will help you remove the balloons from the gelatin bubbles at the end.

Mix the water and gelatin in a microwave-safe bowl until well combined. Allow it to rest for 5 minutes, then microwave it for 10–15 seconds, or until melted. Add the pink food gel and bubblegum flavouring and mix until well combined.

Dip the balloons into the gelatin liquid, making sure they're evenly coated. Leave the bit where the balloon meets the stick free of gelatin. You may want to coat these twice. Let the gelatin set for 5 minutes on the first coat, then dip them again. If the gelatin mixture stiffens, you can melt it again in the microwave for 10 seconds.

Stand the coated balloons upright in a cup or in a Styrofoam block and leave to dry completely.

To remove the bubble from the balloon, cut the balloon away from the straw and pull it out of the bubble. You'll need to trim the bottom of the bubbles to create a neat, level edge so that they sit evenly on top of the frosting. You can do this using a pair of scissors.

Once the bubbles come into contact with any kind of moisture, they will rehydrate and soften again, so it's best to add them to the cake no more than 1 hour before serving.

CUPCAKES

When making the cupcake batter, add the pink food gel and bubblegum flavouring with the wet ingredients. Bake and allow to cool.

BUBBLEGUM GOO

Add all ingredients to a microwave-safe bowl and microwave on high, for 20 seconds at a time, mixing between each interval until smooth. Allow to cool slightly before transferring to a piping bag.

FROSTING & ASSEMBLY

Add the blue food gel and bubblegum flavouring to the frosting and mix until well combined.

To assemble, core the centre of each cupcake with an apple corer (stop about 1 cm (½ in) from the bottom) and fill it with bubblegum goo. Fit the end of a piping bag with a medium round tip, fill the bag with frosting and frost your cupcakes in a flat swirl.

Coat the frosting in the pink sprinkles, starting from the top and working your way around the sides of the frosting. Use the sprinkles to help create a nice bulb shape with your frosting. Finish off by gently placing your gelatin bubble on top.

EASY

MAKES **20** CUPCAKES

20 white cupcake cases

CUPCAKES

1 batch Vanilla cupcakes (page 34)
1 teaspoon melon or grape flavouring
3 drops purple food-gel colouring
3 drops blue food-gel colouring
3 drops pink food-gel colouring
3 drops turquoise food-gel colouring
185 g (6½ oz/1 cup) sprinkles of your choice

FROSTING

1 batch American buttercream frosting (page 45)
3 drops purple food-gel colouring
3 drops blue food-gel colouring
3 drops pink food-gel colouring
3 drops turquoise food-gel colouring
1 teaspoon melon or grape flavouring

GOLD DRIZZLE

2 teaspoons gold lustre dust
80 ml (2½ fl oz/⅓ cup) vodka or vanilla extract

Imagine a royal mermaid wedding under the sea. Now imagine the guests have arrived in the underwater palace hall. Everyone is having a great time swimming around, laughing and catching up with each other while they wait for the new King and Kween to arrive. In they come, and the waiters bring them these cupcakes. These are for a newly married Kween. A Sea Kween.

CUPCAKES

When making the cupcake batter, add the melon flavouring with the wet ingredients.

Divide the batter between four mixing bowls. Colour the first one purple, another blue, another pink and the last one turquoise. Transfer the coloured batters to separate piping bags and snip off the ends.

Pipe little blobs of each coloured batter into each cupcake case, alternating between the four colours until the cases are three-quarters full. Bake, then allow to cool.

FROSTING

Divide the frosting between four small mixing bowls. Colour one purple, another blue, another pink and the last one turquoise. Transfer the coloured frostings to separate piping bags.

Lay out a large sheet of plastic wrap on your workbench and pipe long lines of each coloured frosting in the following order: pink, turquoise, purple and blue.

Use the plastic wrap to help you roll up the frosting like a sushi roll into a log shape, then twist each end to secure. Snip off one end of the log and place it, cut side down, inside a large piping bag fitted with a Wilton 8B tip.

GOLD DRIZZLE

Combine the gold lustre dust and vodka in a small mixing bowl and mix until well combined.

ASSEMBLY

Core the centre of each cupcake with an apple corer (stop about 1 cm (½ in) from the bottom of the cupcake) and fill with sprinkles or a filling of your choice, such as Chocolate sauce (page 51).

Pipe four blobs of frosting on top of each other, making each blob smaller than the last. Finish off with a drizzle of gold lustre paint.

MIDNIGHT GALAXY *cupcakes*

MEDIUM

MAKES **20** CUPCAKES

20 white cupcake cases

CUPCAKES

1 batch Vanilla cupcakes (page 34)
1 teaspoon boysenberry flavouring
black: 5 drops black food-gel colouring and 2 tablespoons unsweetened (Dutch) cocoa powder
turquoise: 2 drops turquoise food-gel colouring
purple: 2 drops purple food-gel colouring and 1 drop black food-gel colouring
185 g (6½ oz/1 cup) galaxy coloured sprinkles (black, green or purple assorted sprinkles)

FROSTING

1 batch Swiss meringue buttercream frosting (page 46)
1 teaspoon boysenberry flavouring
black: 5 drops black food-gel colouring and 2 tablespoons unsweetened (Dutch) cocoa powder
turquoise: 2 drops turquoise food-gel colouring
purple: 2 drops purple food-gel colouring and 1 drop black food-gel colouring

SILVER-STAR SPLATTER

2 teaspoons silver lustre dust
4 teaspoons vodka or vanilla extract
2 tablespoons silver-star sprinkles

There are so many galaxy cupcakes out there, I wanted to put a bit of a dark twist on the popular galaxy trend, hence the moody greens and blues with splatters of twinkling silver stars.

CUPCAKES

When making the cupcake batter, add the boysenberry flavouring with the wet ingredients.

Divide the batter between three bowls. Colour one black, another turquoise and the last one purple using the colour formulations in the ingredients list. The combination of cocoa powder and black food gel allows you to achieve a dark-black colour in almost any batter or frosting. Transfer the coloured batters to separate piping bags and snip off the ends.

Pipe little blobs of each colour into each cupcake case, alternating between the three colours until the cases are three-quarters full. Bake, then allow to cool.

FROSTING

Add the boysenberry flavouring to the frosting and mix until well combined. Divide between three mixing bowls and colour one black, another turquoise and the last one purple. Transfer the coloured frostings to separate piping bags.

Lay out a large sheet of plastic wrap on your workbench and pipe long lines of each coloured frosting on the plastic wrap, starting with black, then blue and then purple.

Use the plastic wrap to help you roll up the frosting like a sushi roll into a log shape, then twist each end to secure. Snip off one end of the log and place it, cut side down, inside a large piping bag fitted with a Wilton 1M tip.

SILVER-STAR SPLATTER

Combine the silver lustre dust and vodka in a bowl and mix until well combined.

ASSEMBLY

Core the centre of each cupcake with an apple corer (stop about 1 cm (½ in) from the bottom of the cupcake) and fill with sprinkles or a filling of your choice, such as Chocolate sauce (page 51), then pipe a tall swirl of frosting on top of each cupcake.

To finish, use a food-safe paintbrush or teaspoon to splatter the frosting on each cupcake with 'silver stars' and finish with a sprinkling of silver-star sprinkles.

HARD

MAKES 20 CUPCAKES

20 white cupcake cases

CUPCAKES

1 batch Vanilla cupcakes (page 34)
2 drops turquoise food-gel colouring
4 drops white food-gel colouring

FROSTING

2 batches American buttercream frosting (page 45)
6 drops pink food-gel colouring
1 teaspoon raspberry or strawberry flavouring

DECORATIONS

20 waffle ice-cream cones
20 red heart sprinkles
60 g (2 oz/⅓ cup) rainbow caviar sprinkles
200 g (7 oz/1 cup) Lucky Charms cereal (or assorted coloured candy, like M&Ms)
90 g (3 oz/2 cups) Lucky Charms marshmallows (or any mini marshmallows of your choice)
12 pink wafer cookies, halved diagonally
20 maraschino cherries, well drained

GANACHE

300 g (10½ oz) white chocolate buttons
50 g (1¾ oz) Wilton turquoise candy melts
100 ml (3½ fl oz) thickened (whipping) cream

When I made this cupcake, I didn't really have a name for it. Whenever that happens, I hop on Instagram and Facebook and ask you guys to name it. 'Sundae Fundae' was the most popular suggestion and I think it works really well. The soft pastel colours remind me of how fun and relaxing Sundays are and how much better they would be with these ice-cream sundae-themed cupcakes!

CUPCAKES

When making the cupcake batter, add the food gels with the wet ingredients. Bake, then allow to cool.

FROSTING

To prepare the frosting, divide three-quarters of the frosting between two separate mixing bowls. Add the pink food gel and raspberry flavouring to one bowl and mix until well combined. Leave the second bowl of frosting plain. Reserve the remaining frosting for filling the ice-cream cones and topping the cake.

Transfer the pink and plain frostings to separate piping bags and snip off the ends. Pipe squiggles of each coloured frosting into a large, deep glass bowl to get a kind of ripple effect, similar to a strawberry- and vanilla-ripple ice cream. Fill the bowl about three-quarters of the way, then gently tap it on a flat surface lined with a folded towel to remove any air bubbles. Refrigerate for 30 minutes to slightly chill. Remove from the fridge 10 minutes before you're ready to use it.

MINI ICE-CREAM CONES

Use a serrated knife to carefully cut the waffle cones into smaller cones, about 3 cm (1¼ in) in length. Using half the reserved frosting, pipe a tall swirl of frosting into each cone. Add a red heart sprinkle on top of the swirl and scatter over some rainbow caviar sprinkles. Sit the frosted ice-cream cones upright in a glass and chill.

GANACHE & ASSEMBLY

To make the ganache, combine all ingredients in a microwave-safe bowl and microwave on high, for 20 seconds at a time, mixing well between each interval until smooth. Allow to cool slightly at room temperature before using, otherwise it will be too thin to drizzle on the cupcakes. Transfer to a piping bag and snip off the end.

To finish the cupcakes, core the centre of each cupcake with an apple corer (stop about 1 cm (½ in) from the bottom of the cupcake) and fill with Lucky Charms cereal. Add some small dabs of ganache to the rim of each cupcake and stick some Lucky Charms marshmallows to it.

The next part is really fun because we use a medium-sized ice-cream scoop to scoop out the rippled frosting the same way you would frozen ice cream. Place a scoop of frosting on top of each cupcake.

Drizzle with the ganache and insert a pink wafer wedge in the frosting. Allow to set.

Fit the end of another piping bag with a small round tip, fill it with the remaining reserved frosting and pipe a swirl of frosting on top of each cupcake before finishing with a maraschino cherry. Push the ice-cream cones into the frosting to stick.

MEDIUM

MAKES 20 CUPCAKES

20 white cupcake cases

GANACHE

300 g (10½ oz) dark chocolate buttons
150 ml (5 fl oz) thickened (whipping) cream

PEACH COOKIES

620 g (1 lb 6 oz) plain (all-purpose) flour
1 tablespoon baking powder
3 large eggs
440 g (15½ oz/2 cups) granulated sugar
185 ml (6 fl oz/¾ cup) full-cream (whole) milk
250 g (9 oz/1 cup) unsalted butter, melted and cooled
zest of 1 orange
80 ml (2½ fl oz/⅓ cup) rum mixed with 2 drops liquid yellow food dye
125 ml (4 fl oz/½ cup) peach liqueur mixed with 2 drops liquid red food dye
fresh mint leaves, to decorate

CUPCAKES

1 batch Vanilla cupcakes (page 34)
80 ml (2½ fl oz/⅓ cup) peach liqueur
2 drops orange food-gel colouring
2 drops pink food-gel colouring
300 g (10½ oz) canned peaches, drained and cubed

FROSTING

1 batch Cream cheese frosting (page 47)

Call Me By Your ... Peach. Fun fact: I hadn't seen that movie until after I made these cupcakes and, when I posted them, everyone went mad in the comments because they thought that the scene from *Call Me By Your Name* was what inspired them. Really what inspired these cupcakes was every pop diva's phat peach bum! If I'm being honest, it was Nicki Minaj. I just wanted to make something to pay tribute to it, and these peach bum cupcakes certainly do that. They also have the fresh flavours of summer. (The cupcakes, that is ...)

GANACHE

To make the ganache, combine the chocolate and cream in a large, microwave-safe bowl. Microwave on high, for 20 seconds at a time, mixing in between each interval until smooth. Set aside at room temperature to set.

PEACH COOKIES

Preheat the oven to 175°C (345°F). Line two baking sheets with baking paper and set aside.

To make the cookies, put the flour and baking powder in a large mixing bowl and whisk together.

Put the eggs in another bowl and whisk until well combined. Add 220 g (8 oz/1 cup) sugar to the whisked eggs and mix to combine.

Next, add the milk, melted butter and orange zest and mix until combined. Add half the flour mixture and stir until smooth, then add the remaining flour mixture and mix until it all comes together. Leave the dough to rest for 5 minutes.

Lightly spray your hands with oil. Roll a tablespoon of the sticky dough between the palms of your hands to form a ball and place it on the baking sheet. Repeat with the rest of the dough, spacing the cookies about 2.5 cm (1 in) apart. Flatten the tops of the cookies slightly with your fingertips.

Bake for 15 minutes, or until the bottoms of the cookies are lightly browned. The tops will remain white.

While the cookies are still warm, use a knife or an apple corer to make a slight hole in the bottom of each cookie. Fill a piping bag with the ganache, snip off the end and fill the cookie holes, but don't overfill them; you don't want the chocolate showing on your peach bums 'cos you know what comes out of those ... Yeah, so don't fill them up too much – just enough to sandwich the cookies together.

Dip half the cookie in the rum mixture and half in the peach liqueur, then dip both sides of the cookies in the remaining sugar to coat, and they're done!

CUPCAKES

When making the cupcake batter, add the peach liqueur and food gels with the wet ingredients.

Once the batter is ready, add the peaches and gently fold them in. Bake for the suggested cooking time plus 15 minutes to account for the extra juice from the peaches. Allow to cool.

ASSEMBLY

Once the cupcakes have cooled, fit a piping bag with a Wilton 6B tip, fill the bag with the frosting and pipe a double-doughnut swirl (see page 14) on each cupcake.

Guys, cream cheese frosting can turn quite soft if it's a warm day. If it is, just use American buttercream frosting (page 45), because when you place the peach bum cookies on top, they can weigh down the frosting, especially if it's too soft. Finish off with a mint leaf on top of the peach right before serving.

HARD

MAKES **10** CUPCAKES

INSPIRED BY: **BLACK VELVET – ALANNAH MYLES**

10 black cupcake cases

BLACK-VELVET CRUMB

1 batch Red velvet cupcakes (page 33)
5 drops black food-gel colouring
1 teaspoon boysenberry flavouring

CUBE-CAKE FROSTING

1 teaspoon boysenberry flavouring
1 batch American buttercream frosting (page 45)

BLACK FROSTING

5 drops black food-gel colouring
½ batch chocolate-flavoured American buttercream frosting (page 45)

CUBE CAKES

2 batches Chocolate cupcakes (page 38)
10 drops black food-gel colouring
1 teaspoon boysenberry flavouring
12 × 6 cm (2½ in) thick cake-pop sticks

CUPCAKES

1 batch Chocolate cupcakes (page 38)
1 teaspoon boysenberry flavouring
8 drops black food-gel colouring

DECORATIONS

1 can pearl food colouring spray

One of the things that really inspire me is architecture. I just love it. I love how it tells a story. I mean, look at how it was used in ancient societies versus how it was used during the industrial revolution versus how it is used today. It changes in style, but the whole philosophy of it changes too. For me, this cupcake is about three things: my love of architecture, minimalism, and how sexy a cupcake can be.

BLACK-VELVET CRUMB

Preheat a fan-forced oven to 140°C (275°F) or a conventional oven to 160°C (320°F). Grease a 40 × 20 cm (16 × 8 in) baking tray with oil spray and line with baking paper. Set aside.

When preparing the cupcake batter, add the black food gel and boysenberry flavouring with the wet ingredients.

Once the batter is ready, pour it into your prepared baking tray. Use a small offset spatula to spread out the batter evenly. Bake for 40 minutes, then leave to cool completely. Reduce the oven temperature to 100°C (212°F).

Once the cake has cooled, add half to a food processor and blitz to very fine crumbs. Transfer the cake crumbs to a mixing bowl and repeat with the other half.

Spread the cake crumbs out over four large baking trays lined with baking paper. Bake for 1 hour, or until the crumbs have dried out and almost resemble dry breadcrumbs. Set aside to cool.

CUBE-CAKE FROSTING

Add the boysenberry flavouring to the frosting and mix until well combined. Set aside.

BLACK FROSTING

Add the black food gel to the frosting and mix until well combined. Set aside.

CUBE CAKES

Preheat a fan-forced oven to 140°C (275°F) or a conventional oven to 160°C (320°F). Grease two 40 × 20 × 6 cm (16 × 8 × 2½ in) baking trays with oil spray and line with baking paper. Set aside.

When making the cupcake batter, add the black food gel and boysenberry flavouring with the wet ingredients.

Once the batter is ready, divide it between the prepared baking trays. Use a small offset spatula to spread out the batter evenly. Bake for 40 minutes, then leave to cool completely.

Once cool, remove the sheets of cake from the baking trays and trim the top of each cake using a cake leveller or large, serrated knife to ensure they are even and flat. Place one of the sheet cakes back in a baking tray. Top with the cube-cake frosting and use a small offset spatula to spread it out evenly. Next, use a cake scraper to spread out the frosting as flat and as evenly as you can.

Carefully place the second sheet cake on top of the frosted cake and gently press down to help it stick to the frosting. Refrigerate for 4 hours.

Once chilled, use a large serrated knife to cut out 5.5 cm (2¼ in) cubes of cake. (Using a ruler will help you make them nice and even.)

Push a cake-pop stick into the corner of each cube, leaving about 3 cm (1¼ in) of the stick sticking out. Transfer to a baking tray and freeze for 1 hour to slightly firm up the cake.

Use a small offset spatula to add a very thin layer of black frosting to all sides of each cube cake, making sure you still retain its sharp edges and corners, then roll the cubes around in the black-velvet crumb. If you find there are any uneven spots or corners on the cake, use your hand to slightly pat down the frosting.

Refrigerate until ready to use.

CUPCAKES & ASSEMBLY

When making the cupcake batter, add the black food gel and boysenberry flavouring with the wet ingredients. Bake, then allow to cool.

To assemble the cupcakes, fit the end of a piping bag with a large round tip, fill it with frosting and pipe a very low swirl on top of each cupcake. Top with the black-velvet crumb.

To finish, insert a cube-cake stick into the centre of each cupcake so that the cubes look like they are just floating above the cakes. Spray them lightly with pearl spray to give them a slight sheen.

See image on page 68.

Note

These cupcakes must be kept chilled. They will collapse in warm environments, so keep them in the fridge until 30 minutes before you want to serve them.

BLACK VELVET *cupcakes*

HIGHWAY UNICORN *cake*

HARD

SERVES **30**

INSPIRED BY: **HIGHWAY UNICORN – LADY GAGA**

CAKE

2 batches Vanilla cake (page 37)
3 teaspoons strawberry flavouring (or any flavouring you like)
blue: 3 drops blue food-gel colouring
purple: 3 drops pink food-gel colouring and 3 drops purple food-gel colouring
pink: 3 drops pink food-gel colouring

HIGHWAY UNICORN MACARONS (OPTIONAL)

1 batch Vanilla macarons (page 42)
1 teaspoon strawberry flavouring
4 drops blue food-gel colouring
4 drops pink food-gel colouring
4 drops purple food-gel colouring

MACARON FROSTING

1 teaspoon strawberry flavouring (or any flavouring you like)
2 drops pink food-gel colouring
1 batch Swiss meringue buttercream frosting (page 46)

This was the second cake I ever made on The Scran Line and it got over 17 million views on Facebook, which is incredible! And I think I know why. It's the definition of over the top. BTW, the inside is as pretty as the outside – check out the image on page 69!

CAKE

When making the batter, add the strawberry flavouring with the wet ingredients.

Divide the batter between three mixing bowls. Add the blue food gel to one bowl, the pink to another and the purple to the last bowl. Mix until well combined.

Transfer each coloured batter to separate piping bags and snip off the ends. Begin by piping about eight blobs of one coloured batter into all three cake tins, then switch to the next colour, alternating between the three colours until you've used all the batter. Bake, then allow to cool.

MACARONS (OPTIONAL)

If you want to use the macarons, I'd recommend making them on the same day you bake the cakes.

When making the meringue for the macarons, add the strawberry flavouring at about the 3-minute mark.

When folding the meringue into the batter, do not mix until the ribbon stage (see page 18). Instead, mix until the meringue and almond mixture are just combined and you can't see any more meringue. It should not be runny.

Divide the mixture between three mixing bowls. Add the blue food gel to one, the pink to another and the purple to the last bowl. Fold each coloured batter until you reach the ribbon stage. Your batter is now ready to pipe.

Spoon about 3 tablespoons of each coloured batter into three separate, medium-sized piping bags. Fit a large piping bag with a medium round tip. Snip the ends off the medium piping bags and place them inside the large piping bag.

Pipe the macarons and top with the sprinkles. Allow to dry, then bake.

CAKE FROSTING

3 teaspoons strawberry flavouring
4 batches Swiss meringue buttercream frosting (page 46)
pink: 6 drops pink food-gel colouring
light purple: 6 drops pink food-gel colouring and 3 drops purple food-gel colouring
purple: 6 drops pink food-gel colouring and 8 drops purple food-gel colouring
blue: 6 drops blue food-gel colouring

DECORATIONS

60 g (2 oz/⅓ cup) white caviar sprinkles
60 g (2 oz/⅓ cup) rainbow jimmies
60 g (2 oz/⅓ cup) rainbow confetti sprinkles

GOLD DRIP

250 ml (8½ fl oz/1 cup) Chocolate sauce (page 51)
2 teaspoons gold lustre dust
80 ml (2½ fl oz/⅓ cup) vodka or vanilla extract

MACARON FROSTING

For the macaron frosting, add the strawberry flavouring and pink food gel to the buttercream and mix until well combined.

Fit the end of a piping bag with a Wilton #32 tip and fill it with the frosting. Pipe a swirl of frosting on the flat side of half the macaron shells, then sandwich with the remaining shells.

CAKE FROSTING

Add the strawberry flavouring to the frosting and mix well.

For the filling and crumb-coat layer, set aside one batch of frosting.

Add the pink food gel to a second batch of frosting and mix until well combined.

Divide the remaining two batches of frosting between three bowls. Colour one light purple, another purple and the last one blue using the colour formulations in the ingredients list.

TO DECORATE

Once the cake has been crumb-coated with the white frosting (see page 10) and has chilled, transfer the pink frosting, light purple, purple and blue frostings to separate, large piping bags. Snip the ends off each one.

Pipe two layers of blue frosting on top of each other around the bottom of the cake. Repeat with the purple, light purple and finish with the pink frosting. Add some more pink frosting to the top of the cake.

Using a small offset spatula, spread the pink frosting on top of the cake. Aim to get it flat. It doesn't have to be perfect because we're going to come back to it.

Use a cake scraper to carefully scrape the frosting around the cake. Scrape any excess frosting off the cake scraper each time you go around the cake to ensure the different layers of coloured frosting stay nice and neat. Continue scraping until the cake is smooth on the side, then gently smooth out the top.

Add some sprinkles around the bottom of the cake, then drizzle the chocolate sauce around the top edge of the cake, letting it drip down the side. This will become your gold drip. Chill for 3 hours.

GOLD DRIP

Once your cake is chilled, mix the gold lustre dust and vodka together and use a small, food-safe paintbrush to carefully paint the chilled chocolate drips gold. You may need to go over it twice. This process can take a while, so be patient. Listen to Beyoncé or your favourite podcast while you paint FOR YOUR LIFE!

Fit the end of a piping bag with a Wilton 1M tip, add the pink frosting and pipe some high swirls on top of the cake. Make 'em high, baby!

Add the macarons on top to finish off, if using.

STUNNING BROWN COW ICE-CREAM *macarons*

MEDIUM

MAKES **15** SANDWICHED MACARONS

ICE CREAM

1.2 litres (41 fl oz) thickened (whipping) cream
250 ml (8½ fl oz/1 cup) sweetened condensed milk
3 teaspoons banana flavouring
120 g (4½ oz) unsweetened (Dutch) cocoa powder
2 ripe bananas, peeled and mashed

MACARONS

1 batch Vanilla macarons (page 42)
5 drops yellow food-gel colouring
1 teaspoon banana flavouring

CHOCOLATE PAINT

50 g (1¾ oz) unsweetened (Dutch) cocoa powder

Now, you may be thinking to yourself that these look an awful lot more like a giraffe than a brown cow ... There was an episode of *Drag Race* where one of the queens (Monique Heart) wore a giraffe-print outfit for a runway challenge and, when the judge told her they were confused about why she was wearing a giraffe pattern for the challenge, she said she thought it was a brown cow. Monique's iconic response was: 'I saw it and I was like, ah, brown cow! Stunning!' And here it is. The stunning brown cow macaron in honour of Monique's brown-cow outfit, because inside every giraffe is a brown cow.

ICE CREAM

Line a 20 × 30 × 5 cm (8 × 12 × 2 in) baking tin with plastic wrap. Set aside.

Add the cream, sweetened condensed milk and banana flavouring to a large mixing bowl, then use a hand mixer to whisk the mixture to soft peaks. Add the cocoa powder and continue whisking to stiff peaks. Fold in the mashed banana.

Pour the mixture into the prepared tin and use a large offset spatula to spread it out evenly. Cover with plastic wrap and freeze for 5 hours, or overnight.

MACARONS

When making the meringue for the macarons, add the yellow food gel and banana flavouring at about the 3-minute mark.

Pipe the macarons about 5 cm (2 in) in diameter (you need to pipe 30 shells to be sandwiched), then dry and bake.

CHOCOLATE PAINT

To make the chocolate paint, combine the cocoa powder with about 100 ml (3½ fl oz) water in a mixing bowl and whisk until combined. You're looking for a dripping consistency: not so thick that it won't splatter, and not so thin that it becomes translucent. Add a little extra water if needed to achieve the right consistency.

Once the macarons have baked and cooled, use a new toothbrush to dip into the chocolate paint and splatter it onto the macaron shells by flicking the toothbrush with your finger. Once all the macaron shells are covered, leave to dry for 3 hours.

ASSEMBLY

To prepare the chocolate ice cream, remove the tin from the freezer and take off the plastic wrap. Using a round 5 cm (2 in) cookie cutter, cut out discs of ice cream.

Place an ice-cream disc on the flat side of half the macaron shells, then sandwich with the remaining shells.

'Hey Nick, do you think you'll ever run out of ideas?'

I've designed over 300 cupcakes in four years. If I was going to run out, I would have run out by now. But here's the secret ...

As long as I feel inspired by something, I can never run out of ideas. Not to toot my own horn, but I've worked hard to gain the skills that allow me to make cupcakes and think about desserts in a way that nobody else can.

Everyone has the skill to use what inspires them and turn it into something wonderful. The difference between me and everyone else is that most people haven't figured out how to access that part of themselves yet. And it was no easy road getting to the point where I could make a cupcake inspired by literally anything. You just have to keep trying and practising the thing you're passionate about.

Here's a collection of some of my favourite designs (and yours) to prove that! In this chapter, you'll find classic flavours like salted caramel, recipes to help you celebrate the first day of spring, Mother's Day, or desserts inspired by countries like France and Italy. You name it, it's in this collection. Variety is the spice of life, and this chapter is spicy!

VEGAN COOKIES AND CREAM *cupcakes*

EASY

MAKES **12** CUPCAKES

12 white cupcake cases

VEGAN FROSTING

200 g (7 oz) butter-flavoured Crisco shortening
100 g (3½ oz) dairy-free/vegan margarine
350 g (12½ oz) icing (confectioners') sugar
200 g (7 oz/1 cup) crushed Oreo cookies

CUPCAKES

160 g (5½ oz) plain (all-purpose) flour
170 g (6 oz/¾ cup) caster (superfine) sugar
40 g (1½ oz/⅓ cup) unsweetened (Dutch) cocoa powder
¾ teaspoon bicarbonate of soda (baking soda)
½ teaspoon baking powder
¼ teaspoon fine salt
250 ml (8½ fl oz/1 cup) coconut milk
175 ml (6 fl oz) canola oil
1½ teaspoons apple-cider vinegar

DECORATIONS

200 g (7 oz/1 cup) roughly chopped Oreo cookies
200 g (7 oz) dairy-free or vegan chocolate, melted

Guys, I don't mess around when it comes to cookies-and-cream flavours. I'm usually not a fan of cookies and cream–flavoured cakes. It's because whoever makes them doesn't add enough cookies to be able to actually taste the cookie. Not in my recipe! Mine may as well just be a cup of cookies, but then it wouldn't be a cupcake! These cupcakes won't disappoint if you're like me and want something to actually taste like the thing it says it is.

FROSTING

Add the shortening and margarine to a large mixing bowl and whip for 5 minutes until it turns pale in colour. Using a stand mixer makes this process easier, but you can use a hand mixer too.

Add the icing sugar and crushed Oreos and mix on low speed until all the dry ingredients have been incorporated. Turn the mixer back up to high speed and whip for 10 minutes.

CUPCAKES

Preheat a fan-forced oven to 140°C (275°F) or a conventional oven to 160°C (320°F). Line a cupcake tin with white cupcake cases.

Add the flour, sugar, cocoa powder, bicarbonate of soda, baking powder and salt to a large mixing bowl and mix well using a hand mixer.

Next, add the coconut milk, canola oil and apple-cider vinegar. Mix on low speed until all the dry ingredients have been incorporated. Scrape down the side of the bowl and mix on low speed for a final 20 seconds.

Fill each cupcake case three-quarters of the way with mixture. Using an ice-cream scoop to transfer the batter to the cases makes this a quick and easy process and ensures the cupcakes are the same size so they bake evenly. Bake for 40–50 minutes, or until a toothpick inserted in the centre of a cupcake comes out clean. I bake my cupcakes slowly on a low temperature. This ensures they don't colour and crack on top. Allow the cupcakes to cool completely on a wire rack before frosting.

ASSEMBLY

To finish, fit a piping bag with a large round tip, fill with the frosting and pipe a large bulb on top of each cupcake. Place some roughly chopped Oreos on top and drizzle with the melted chocolate.

VEGAN CHOCOLATE RASPBERRY *cake*

MEDIUM

SERVES **30**

OK, so I've always said this, but my vegan chocolate cake and cupcake recipe is (IMO) better than my regular chocolate cake recipe. This cake comes out so moist, it's amazing! You can pretty much adapt it to make any flavoured chocolate cake you like: chocolate coffee, vegan snickers – anything! If you're looking for some ideas, I have heaps on my website.

VEGAN CHOCOLATE FROSTING

500 g (1 lb 2 oz/2 cups) butter-flavoured Crisco shortening
300 g (10½ oz) dairy-free/vegan margarine
1 kg (2 lb 3 oz/8 cups) icing (confectioners') sugar
250 g (9 oz/2 cups) unsweetened (Dutch) cocoa powder
4 teaspoons raspberry flavouring

CAKE

320 g (11½ oz) plain (all-purpose) flour
350 g (12½ oz) caster (superfine) sugar
80 g (2¾ oz) unsweetened (Dutch) cocoa powder
1½ teaspoons bicarbonate of soda (baking soda)
1 teaspoon baking powder
½ teaspoon fine salt
500 ml (17 fl oz/2 cups) coconut milk
250 ml (8½ fl oz/1 cup) canola oil
3 teaspoons apple-cider vinegar
400 g (14 oz/2 cups) frozen raspberries
150 g (5½ oz/1 cup) crushed freeze-dried raspberries

Please note: To make the six-layered cake as shown in the image on page 80, you'll need to make two batches of the cake batter, and two batches of frosting to fill, crumb-coat, frost and decorate the cake.

VEGAN CHOCOLATE FROSTING

Add the shortening and margarine to a large mixing bowl and whip for 5 minutes until it turns pale in colour. Using a stand mixer makes this process easier, but you can use a hand mixer instead.

Add 125 g (4½ oz/1 cup) of the icing sugar, the cocoa powder and raspberry flavouring, and mix on low speed. Continue adding the rest of the icing sugar, 125 g (4½ oz/1 cup) at a time. Once all the dry ingredients have been incorporated, turn the mixer back up to high speed and whip for another 10 minutes.

CAKE

Preheat a fan-forced oven to 140°C (275°F) or a conventional oven to 160°C (320°F). Grease three 20 cm (8 in) cake tins with oil spray and line the bottoms with baking paper (see page 10) for the six-layer cake. Set aside.

Add the flour, sugar, cocoa powder, bicarbonate of soda, baking powder and salt to a large mixing bowl and mix with a hand mixer until well combined.

Next, add the coconut milk, canola oil and apple-cider vinegar and mix on low speed until all the dry ingredients have been incorporated. Scrape down the side of the bowl, add the frozen raspberries and fold them into the batter.

Divide the cake mixture between the three tins. I find using an ice-cream scoop makes it easy to distribute the batter evenly, ensuring the cakes bake at the same rate.

Because of the added moisture from the raspberries, this cake will take a long time to bake. Don't panic though; it will still come out delicate and moist. Bake the cakes for 1½ hours, or until a toothpick inserted in the centre of a cake comes out clean. If the toothpick comes out coated in wet batter, continue baking, for 10 minutes at a time, until fully baked. Allow the cakes to cool to room temperature in the tins, then cover in plastic wrap and chill in the fridge overnight, still in their tins.

To trim, fill and crumb-coat your cake, see page 10.

To frost your cake, see page 12. Reserve a small amount of frosting for the decoration stage (see below).

TO DECORATE

Stick the freeze-dried raspberries around the sides of the cake, reserving some for the top. Start off with a heavy layer at the bottom, then add fewer and fewer as you work towards the top to get a kind of ombre effect.

Fit the end of a piping bag with a Wilton 1M tip, fill it with the reserved chocolate frosting and pipe swirls of frosting on top of the cake. Finish with more freeze-dried raspberries.

See image on page 80.

***VEGAN CHOCOLATE RASPBERRY** cake*

WHEN MACARON MET CUPCAKE *cupcakes*

EASY

MAKES **10** CUPCAKES

10 white cupcake cases

MACARONS

1 batch Vanilla macarons (page 42)
10 drops deep pink food-gel colouring
1 teaspoon raspberry flavouring
1 batch Chocolate ganache frosting, whipped (page 49)

CUPCAKES

1 batch Chocolate cupcakes (page 38)

CREAM TOPPING (SEE NOTE)

250 ml (8½ fl oz/1 cup) thickened (whipping) cream
1 teaspoon vanilla extract

DECORATIONS

½ batch Chocolate sauce (page 51)
12 maraschino cherries, well drained

Note

If it's a warm day, you can replace the cream topping with American buttercream frosting (page 45), which will hold better.

This was bound to happen at some point. One day, I baked some chocolate cupcakes and some pink macaron shells ready to decorate the next day for a different recipe. I got up the next morning and I caught the two of them in the throes of passion on the kitchen bench. Nine months later, out popped this cupcake. It was a match made in heaven.

MACARONS

When making the meringue for the macarons, add the pink food gel and raspberry flavouring at about the 3-minute mark. Scrape down the side of the bowl at least once to ensure the meringue is evenly coloured.

When piping the macarons, pipe them slightly smaller than the diameter of the cupcakes. You'll need 24 macaron shells. Allow to dry, then bake.

To assemble the macarons, fit the end of a piping bag with a Wilton 6B tip, fill with the chocolate ganache and pipe a swirl of ganache on the flat side of half the shells. Sandwich with the remaining shells.

CUPCAKES

Make one batch of chocolate cupcakes. Bake, then allow to cool.

CREAM TOPPING

Combine the cream and vanilla extract in a large metal or glass mixing bowl. Whisk on high speed using a hand mixer until stiff peaks form. Cover with plastic wrap and refrigerate until ready to use.

ASSEMBLY

Core the centre of each cupcake with an apple corer (stop about 1 cm (½ in) from the bottom) and fill with chocolate sauce.

Pipe three small blobs of ganache on top of each cupcake and stick a macaron on top.

Fit the end of a piping bag with an open-star tip, fill it with cream topping and pipe a small swirl of cream on top. Finish with a maraschino cherry just before serving.

See image on page 81.

MEDIUM

MAKES **20** CUPCAKES

20 white cupcake cases

CRÈME PÂTISSIÈRE

4 teaspoons powdered gelatin
6 egg yolks
1 teaspoon vanilla bean paste
100 g (3½ oz) granulated sugar
2 tablespoons cornflour (cornstarch)
2 tablespoons plain (all-purpose) flour
500 ml (17 fl oz/2 cups) hot full-cream (whole) milk
300 g (10½ oz) cold butter, cubed

CHOUX PASTRY

125 g (4½ oz/½ cup) unsalted butter, cut into small dice
1 teaspoon caster (superfine) sugar
½ teaspoon fine salt
220 g (8 oz) plain (all-purpose) flour
4–5 eggs
egg wash (1 egg whisked with 2 teaspoons milk)
100 g (3½ oz) flaked almonds (optional)

CUPCAKES

1 batch Vanilla cupcakes (page 34)
1 teaspoon vanilla bean paste

DECORATIONS

icing (confectioners') sugar, for dusting

CONTINUED ON PAGE 84

I am ob-SESSED with French pastries. In fact, I made the decision to become a pastry chef after a two-week trip to Paris where I fell in love with all the amazing food. This French pastry filled with crème pâtissière is traditionally about the size of a dinner plate, but here it is in cupcake form!

CRÈME PÂTISSIÈRE

For all you purists out there, I know traditional crème pâtissière doesn't include gelatin, but this recipe uses it to help stabilise the crème so that it's firm enough to pipe.

Begin by adding the gelatin to a small, microwave-safe bowl with 160 ml (5½ fl oz) cold water. Give it a stir and set aside to bloom.

Combine the egg yolks, vanilla bean paste and sugar in a large mixing bowl and whisk until the mixture turns lighter in colour.

Add the cornflour and plain flour, and stir until the mixture is smooth. Add one-third of the hot milk and stir until well combined, then slowly add the rest of the milk, stirring constantly.

Transfer the mixture to a saucepan and stir over a medium heat until it thickens and becomes smooth. It has reached the right consistency when it coats the back of a spoon. If you can run a finger through it and leave a clean line, it's ready to take off the heat.

Microwave the gelatin mixture on high for 15 seconds. Add the melted gelatin to the hot custard and stir until it dissolves completely, then add the cold butter cubes and stir until melted and combined.

Transfer the custard to a bowl, cover with plastic wrap and chill for at least 3–4 hours or overnight to allow it to completely set. When you're ready to pipe, gently stir the custard until smooth.

CHOUX PASTRY

Combine the butter, sugar and salt in a saucepan with 250 ml (8½ fl oz/1 cup) water and bring to the boil over a medium heat. Once boiling, remove the pan from the heat and add the flour. Beat with a wooden spoon until a soft dough forms.

Put the saucepan back over a medium heat and stir continuously. A couple of things are happening while you do this: the mixture is being cooked, but it's also drying out. You'll notice a lot of steam coming out of the dough as you mix it. That's what you want to happen. This step can get quite tiring, but push past the pain and stir! This is the way it's been done for centuries, and plenty of chefs before you have survived.

After about 2–3 minutes, the mixture will begin to pull away from the side of the pan and a film will form on the bottom. Once that happens, remove it from the heat.

Transfer the hot dough to a large mixing bowl and leave it to cool for 5 minutes. Using a hand mixer or a wooden spoon, start adding the eggs, one at a time, mixing well between each addition.

After you have added the fourth egg, test to see if the mixture is sticky enough. The best way to do this is by stretching it out between two fingers. If it stretches without breaking, then it's done. If it's too dry, add the fifth egg.

Preheat a fan-forced oven to 220°C (430°F) or a conventional oven to 240°C (450°F). Add a dab of sticky dough to the corners of two baking trays, then line with baking paper.

Fit the end of a piping bag with a medium round tip, fill with the dough and pipe out small rings, about 5–6 cm (2–2½ in) in diameter. Use your fingers to brush the rings with the egg wash, then sprinkle each ring with flaked almonds.

Bake for 10 minutes, then reduce the oven temperature to 175°C (345°F) for a fan-forced oven (195°C/365°F for a conventional oven) and bake until golden brown. Transfer the baked pastries to a wire rack and allow to cool before slicing them in half with a serrated knife.

CUPCAKES

When making the batter for the cupcakes, add the vanilla bean paste with the wet ingredients instead of the vanilla extract. For classic French sweets, I like to use vanilla bean paste because it has a stronger flavour and the little flecks of vanilla seeds make it feel extra special. Bake, then allow to cool.

ASSEMBLY

To thin out some crème pâtissière for piping, add 175 ml (6 fl oz) warm milk to 250 ml (8½ fl oz/1 cup) warm crème pâtissière and whisk until well combined. Transfer to a piping bag and snip off the end.

To assemble the cupcakes, core each cupcake with an apple corer (stop about 1 cm (½ in) from the bottom) and fill with the thinned-out crème pâtissière. Fit another piping bag with a Wilton 6B tip, fill it with thick crème patisserie and pipe small blobs around the edge of the cored centres. Place a choux pastry ring on top, pressing it very gently into the thick crème patisserie to hold it in place. Pipe a swirl of thick crème pâtissière on top of each choux ring, then sandwich with the remaining rings and dust with icing sugar just before serving.

Note

These cupcakes are best assembled on the day you want to serve them. You can prepare the cupcakes, crème pâtissière and the choux pastry rings the day before.

SALTED CARAMEL cupcakes

EASY

MAKES **10** CUPCAKES

10 white cupcake cases

CUPCAKES

1 batch Chocolate cupcakes (page 38)
1 batch Salted caramel sauce (page 50)

FROSTING

1 batch American buttercream frosting (page 45)
125 ml (4 fl oz/½ cup) Salted caramel sauce (page 50)

I was never a fan of caramel anything before I tried my first salted caramel cupcake, because the difference with these and anything else caramel is the salt. It really intensifies the caramel flavour and makes these cupcakes less sweet and just pure indulgent.

CUPCAKES

Prepare and bake the cupcakes, then allow to cool.

FROSTING

Prepare the frosting, then fit the end of a piping bag with a Wilton 1M tip and fill with the frosting.

ASSEMBLY

Core the centre of each cupcake with an apple corer (stop about 1 cm (½ in) from the bottom) and fill with the salted caramel sauce. Pipe a swirl of frosting on top of the cupcakes. Drizzle with the salted caramel sauce.

NEAPOLITAN *cupcakes*

EASY

MAKES **20** CUPCAKES

20 white cupcake cases

FROSTING

1 batch American buttercream frosting (page 45)
40 g (1½ oz) unsweetened (Dutch) cocoa powder
3 drops pink food-gel colouring
1 teaspoon strawberry flavouring

CUPCAKES

1 batch Vanilla cupcakes (page 34)
40 g (1½ oz) unsweetened (Dutch) cocoa powder
3 drops pink food-gel colouring
1 teaspoon strawberry flavouring

DECORATIONS

250 ml (8½ fl oz/1 cup) Chocolate sauce (page 51)
20 maraschino cherries, well drained

My first memories of Neapolitan ice cream are from visiting my grandma's house. She'd always have it in the freezer for us. Most people went for the chocolate ice cream, but you can have chocolate any day. Personally, I went for the strawberry ice cream. I'd put a little chocolate and vanilla in there too, then I'd sit at the table next to my brother and we'd mix it all together until it became one big, grey milkshake that we'd eat like soup. Don't ask me why, but that's still how I eat Neapolitan ice cream.

FROSTING

Make the frosting, then divide it between three mixing bowls. Add the cocoa powder to one bowl and mix until well combined. Next, add the pink food gel and strawberry flavouring to the second bowl and mix. Leave the third bowl plain. Set aside.

CUPCAKES

Once the batter is ready, repeat the same flavouring and colouring process as for the frosting.

Transfer the flavoured batters to separate piping bags and snip off the ends. Fill your cupcake cases about three-quarters of the way with batter, alternating between the three colours. Add the chocolate to the bottom, followed by the strawberry, and finish with vanilla. Bake, then allow to cool.

ASSEMBLY

Core the centre of each cupcake with an apple corer (stop about 1 cm (½ in) from the bottom) and fill with chocolate sauce.

To finish your cupcakes, fit a piping bag with an open-star tip and fill with chocolate frosting. Repeat with the strawberry and vanilla frosting. Pipe a flat swirl of chocolate frosting on top of each cupcake. Next, pipe a slightly smaller swirl of strawberry frosting on top of that and, finally, a swirl of vanilla frosting. Finish with a maraschino cherry.

EASY

MAKES 20 CUPCAKES

20 white cupcake cases

FROSTING

1 teaspoon vanilla bean paste
3 tablespoons mascarpone cheese
1 batch Cream cheese frosting (page 47)

COFFEE MIXTURE

3 tablespoons instant coffee
125 ml (4 fl oz/½ cup) boiling water

CUPCAKES

1 batch Vanilla cupcakes (page 34)
1 teaspoon vanilla bean paste

DECORATIONS

1 batch Chocolate sauce (page 51)
40 g (1½ oz) sweetened cocoa powder

The first time I had tiramisu (that wasn't my mum's) was in Italy. If you ever go to Italy (shout-out to my Italian followers), there are several things you should eat while you are there: pizza, pasta and tiramisu. The first time I ever went to Italy I was about 12 and my mum's dream was to go to Venice. As soon as we touched down in Rome, we lost her at the airport. An hour later, she came back with pizza for all of us. It was delicious.

I visited Italy for the second time when I was 24. I spent the last day in Florence. I suddenly remembered the promise I had made myself: to try real Italian tiramisu. I've been a fan ever since. The combination of vanilla cake, strong coffee and rich mascarpone cream-cheese frosting with a hint of chocolate will give you some serious food-coma vibes. This is my second favourite cupcake flavour of all time after red velvet.

FROSTING

To prepare the frosting, add the vanilla bean paste and mascarpone cheese to the frosting and mix until well combined. Beat the mixture on high speed, using either a stand mixer or a hand mixer, until fluffy.

COFFEE MIXTURE

Mix the instant coffee and boiling water in a small bowl until the coffee has dissolved.

CUPCAKES

When making the cupcake batter, replace the vanilla extract with the vanilla bean paste.

Once the cupcakes are baked and cooled, dip the tops into the coffee mixture, allowing it to soak in and drip down the sides of the cupcakes. Take care not to soak them too much, otherwise you'll risk the cupcake cases coming away from the cakes.

ASSEMBLY

Core the centre of each cupcake with an apple corer (stop about 1 cm (½ in) from the bottom) and fill it with chocolate sauce.

Fit the end of a piping bag with a Wilton 1M tip, fill it with frosting and pipe a swirl of frosting on top of each cake. Finish with a dusting of cocoa powder.

DOUBLE-STACK OREO *cake*

HARD

SERVES **45**

Recipe can be halved or quartered.

FROSTING

4 batches Swiss meringue buttercream frosting (page 46)
200 g (7 oz) crushed Oreos

CAKE

3 batches Vanilla cake (page 37)
500 g (1 lb 2 oz) Oreos, roughly chopped

DECORATIONS

5 bubble straws or plastic dowel rods
400 g (14 oz) Oreos, roughly chopped (for filling the cake)
1 batch Chocolate ganache frosting, unwhipped (page 49)
200 g (7 oz) Oreos (broken into a mixture of large chunks and small chunks, and some crushed)
1 batch Chocolate sauce (page 51)
6 whole Oreos (to top the cake)

My fave thing about this cake is the cookie ombre. It's really easy to do and it looks awesome. Serve a slice of this cake with a glass of milk, but do not dunk!

FROSTING

Set aside about 300 g (10½ oz) of plain frosting for the swirls on top of the cake, and flavour the rest with the crushed Oreos. Mix until well combined, then transfer to a piping bag and snip off the end.

CAKE

This cake is quite large, so it will need to be made in three separate batches. For the 20 cm (8 in) cake, you'll need a thick 20 cm (8 in) cake board. For the 15 cm (6 in) cake, you'll need a thin 15 cm (6 in) cake board.

Make the three batches of cake batter, divide the chopped Oreos evenly between each batch and fold in until well combined.

Divide two batches of the batter between three 20 cm (8 in) cake tins and the last batch of batter between two 15 cm (6 in) cake tins. Bake, then allow to cool.

Once the cakes have cooled, cut each of the large cakes in half with a large, serrated knife. This will give you six 20 cm (8 in) cake layers. Do the same with the two smaller cakes to create four 15 cm (6 in) cake layers.

To fill your cakes, place a small dab of Oreo frosting on the larger cake board and top with one of the 20 cm (8 in) cakes. Add a layer of Oreo buttercream on top, followed by a sprinkling of chopped Oreos. Continue layering the cakes, frosting and Oreos until all of the large cakes have been used. To fill the smaller cakes, put the ganache in a piping bag and snip off the end. Add a dab of ganache to the smaller cake board and top with one of the 15 cm (6 in) cakes. Add a layer of chocolate ganache in between each of the cake layers.

Crumb-coat both cakes with the Oreo frosting (see page 10), then chill overnight. Once chilled, add the top layer of Oreo frosting to both cakes (see page 12).

TO DECORATE

So now, the fun part: putting it all together! So that the larger cake doesn't collapse when the smaller cake is placed on top, you'll need to add some support beams to the larger cake. You can use bubble straws or plastic dowel rods for this, both of which can be found at your local cake supply store or online. You'll need five straws in total.

Start by sticking one straw into the larger cake. When it hits the bottom, lift it slightly and use a food-safe marker to mark where the straw sits level with the top of the cake. Remove the straw and use the marked straw to cut the remaining straws.

Stick one straw in the centre of the cake, pushing it all the way in. Be patient and don't push too hard, otherwise you'll leave a punch mark in the top of your beautiful cake. Push in the remaining four straws, evenly spaced around the cake.

Add a dab of frosting to the top of your larger cake and, using a large offset spatula, carefully place the smaller cake – sitting on its cake board – on top.

Press the Oreo chunks onto the outside of both cakes, starting with the larger chunks at the bottom, followed by the smaller chunks, and finishing with smaller crushed Oreo pieces at the top to create an ombre effect.

Fit the end of a piping bag with a Wilton 6B tip and fill it with the reserved plain frosting. Pipe six swirls on top of the smaller cake and drizzle with the chocolate sauce. Top each swirl with a whole Oreo to finish.

See image on page 94.

DOUBLE-STACK OREO *cake*

GIANT FUNFETTI COOKIE DOUGH *cake*

GIANT FUNFETTI COOKIE DOUGH *cake*

HARD

SERVES **45**

VANILLA COOKIE LAYER

125 g (4½ oz/½ cup) unsalted butter, softened
110 g (4 oz) firmly packed dark brown sugar
90 g (3 oz) granulated sugar
1 large egg
2 tablespoons full-cream (whole) milk
1 teaspoon vanilla extract
470 g (1 lb 1 oz) dark chocolate chips
1 teaspoon bicarbonate of soda (baking soda)
½ teaspoon fine salt
200 g (7 oz/1⅓ cups) plain (all-purpose) flour

CHOCOLATE COOKIE LAYER

125 g (4½ oz/½ cup) unsalted butter, softened
110 g (4 oz) firmly packed dark brown sugar
90 g (3 oz) granulated sugar
1 large egg
2 tablespoons full-cream (whole) milk
1 teaspoon vanilla extract
230 g (8 oz) milk chocolate chips
230 g (8 oz) white chocolate chips
1 teaspoon bicarbonate of soda (baking soda)
½ teaspoon fine salt
200 g (7 oz/ 1⅓ cups) plain (all-purpose) flour
60 g (2 oz/½ cup) unsweetened (Dutch) cocoa powder

Want a challenge? Look no further! Here's the truth: most of the time I have a clear idea in my head of how a recipe is going to work. The majority of the time things go right, except for this recipe. It just kept going and going and, before I knew it, I needed more frosting, then even more frosting, all sandwiched by a vanilla cookie layer, chocolate cookie layer, vanilla cake and chocolate cake! It just kept growing in front of my eyes into a delicious giant cake.

Please note: This recipe will need to be made over at least 2 days to allow the cakes and cookie layers to cool completely overnight. Once you've made all the layers, you'll have six layers all up: 1 vanilla cookie layer, 1 chocolate cookie layer, 2 vanilla cake layers and 2 chocolate cake layers.

VANILLA AND CHOCOLATE COOKIE LAYERS

Each recipe will yield one 20 cm (8 in) cookie.

Preheat the oven to 180°C (350°F). Spray two 20 cm (8 in) cake tins with oil and line the bottoms with baking paper (see page 10). Set aside.

Prepare the cookie doughs separately. Beat the butter, brown sugar and granulated sugar with a hand mixer until well combined and pale in colour, about 2 minutes.

Add the egg, milk and vanilla extract, and mix on low speed until well combined.

Add the chocolate chips and mix again, then add the bicarbonate of soda, salt and half of the flour. Mix until well combined, then add the remaining flour and the cocoa powder (for the chocolate cookie) and mix well.

Transfer the cookie doughs to the prepared cake tins and pat the dough flat with clean hands. Bake for 30 minutes, then allow to cool at room temperature before removing from the tins.

VANILLA AND CHOCOLATE CAKE LAYERS

Each recipe will yield one 20 cm (8 in) cake.

Once both cake batters are ready, fold the dark chocolate chips into the vanilla batter and fold the white and milk chocolate chips into the chocolate batter.

Add the vanilla batter to one prepared cake tin and the chocolate batter to the other. Bake for 1½ hours, then allow to cool completely in the tins.

To trim the cakes, see page 10.

VANILLA CAKE LAYER

1 batch Vanilla cake (page 37)
175 g (6 oz/1 cup) dark chocolate chips

CHOCOLATE CAKE LAYER

½ batch Chocolate cake (page 41)
175 g (6 oz/1 cup) white chocolate chips
175 g (6 oz/1 cup) milk chocolate chips

COOKIE DOUGH

60 g (2 oz/¼ cup) unsalted butter, softened
85 g (3 oz) firmly packed brown sugar
1 teaspoon vanilla extract
175 ml (6 fl oz) full-cream (whole) milk (you might not need all of the milk)
125 g (4½ oz) chocolate chips (milk, dark or white)
¼ teaspoon fine salt
100 g (3½ oz/⅔ cup) plain (all-purpose) flour

MOLASSES FROSTING

80 ml (2½ fl oz/⅓ cup) molasses
2 batches Swiss meringue buttercream frosting (page 46)

STRAWBERRY FROSTING

10 drops pink food-gel colouring
4 teaspoons strawberries and cream flavouring (or any flavouring you like)
2 batches Swiss meringue buttercream frosting (page 46)

DECORATIONS

185 g (6½ oz/1 cup) rainbow jimmies
185 g (6½ oz) mini chocolate chips
1 batch Chocolate sauce (page 51)
10 small, store-bought choc-chip cookies (to top the cake)

COOKIE DOUGH

Combine the butter and sugar in a large mixing bowl and cream together using a hand mixer until pale and fluffy.

Stir in the vanilla extract, milk and chocolate chips.

Add the salt and half of the flour and mix until well combined. Add the remaining flour and mix well. The mixture should have the consistency of a firm paste. If you feel it's too dry, add a little more milk, 1 tablespoon at a time, until you reach the right consistency.

Divide the mixture in half. Roll one half of the mixture into small balls about 1 teaspoon in size. Refrigerate until ready to use. You'll use the other half of the mixture in between each cake layer.

MOLASSES FROSTING

Add the molasses to the frosting and mix until well combined. You'll use this frosting to fill and crumb-coat the cake.

STRAWBERRY FROSTING

Add the pink food gel and strawberry flavouring to the frosting and mix until well combined. You'll use this frosting for the final layer of the cake and to decorate the top.

TO DECORATE

To assemble the cake, fill a piping bag with the molasses frosting and snip off the end. Add a dab of the frosting to a thick 20 cm (8 in) cake board or flat serving plate. Add the chocolate cookie layer, then pipe a ring of frosting around the top edge. Pipe more frosting in the middle and use a small offset spatula to spread it out. Top with little bits of cookie dough.

Next, add the vanilla cookie. Repeat the process with the molasses frosting and cookie dough. Add the first chocolate cake, followed by the first vanilla cake, then the second chocolate cake and, finally, the second vanilla cake, layering them with the molasses frosting.

To crumb-coat the cake, see page 10. Chill for 3 hours.

Add most of the strawberry frosting to a piping bag and snip off the end. Use this frosting to add the final layer to your cake (see page 12).

Once frosted, stick some balls of cookie dough around the bottom of the cake, followed by some rainbow jimmies and mini chocolate chips.

Drizzle the top edge of the cake with the chocolate sauce. Fit the end of a piping bag with a Wilton 8B tip, fill it with the remaining strawberry frosting and pipe small bulbs of frosting on the top of the cake, then pile the store-bought choc-chip cookies in the middle of the cake.

See image on page 95.

CACTUS GARDEN *cake*

Here's an example of a cake trend that I ignored and came back to once it was over, with my own twist and take on it. When I was coming up with this cake design, I didn't want the cacti to look real. I wanted them to look bright, colourful and almost like they were inspired by a cartoon alien planet.

HARD

SERVES **30**

TEAL GANACHE DRIZZLE

150 g (5½ oz) white chocolate buttons
75 ml (2½ fl oz) thickened (whipping) cream
1 drop teal food-gel colouring

RASPBERRY FROSTING

160 g (5½ oz/½ cup) raspberry jam
1 teaspoon raspberry flavouring (optional)
2 drops pink food-gel colouring
1½ batches Swiss meringue buttercream frosting (page 46)

STRIPED FROSTING

1 batch Swiss meringue buttercream frosting (page 46)
peach: 3 drops pink food-gel colouring and 3 drops orange food-gel colouring

TEAL GANACHE DRIZZLE

Combine the white chocolate and cream in a large, microwave-safe bowl. Microwave on high for 20 seconds at a time, mixing between each interval until smooth. Add a drop of teal food gel and mix until well combined. Cover with plastic wrap and set aside at room temperature.

Alternatively, you can make the ganache using the double-boiler method. Fill a large saucepan one-third of the way with water and bring to the boil. Place the bowl containing the chocolate and cream on top and gently mix until the two ingredients are completely melted and smooth.

To soften the ganache to drizzling consistency, microwave on high, for 5 seconds at a time, mixing well in between each interval. Dip a spoon into the ganache and, if it drizzles down and doesn't look transparent, it's ready to use on the cake.

RASPBERRY FROSTING

Add the raspberry jam, raspberry flavouring (if using) and the pink food gel to the buttercream and mix with a hand mixer until well combined. This is the frosting you'll use to fill and crumb-coat the cake.

STRIPED FROSTING

Divide the frosting between two bowls. To make the peach frosting, colour one bowl with the orange and pink food gel and mix until well combined. Leave the other bowl white.

CACTUS DECORATIONS

Check out the image on page 100 to guide you in creating the cacti. Begin by lining two baking trays with baking paper. Set aside.

Set about 3 tablespoons of the American buttercream frosting aside. This is your plain white frosting.

Colour one-quarter of the remaining frosting teal, and another one-quarter of the frosting lime-green. Divide the remaining frosting between three mixing bowls and colour them pink, peach and purple following the colouring formulations in the ingredients list.

For the large and small bulb cacti, use your hands to mould a small log out of one of the Rice Krispie bars. Aim to get one end of the log a little flatter than the other. Fit the end of a piping bag with a Wilton #32 tip and fill it with the lime-green frosting. Add a small bulb of lime-green frosting to the bottom of the Rice Krispie log and stick it to a baking tray. Pipe lines around the log, starting at the bottom and working your way to the top. Continue until the cactus is completely frosted.

CACTUS DECORATIONS

1 batch American buttercream frosting (page 45)
teal: 5 drops teal food-gel colouring
lime-green: 4 drops teal food-gel colouring and 4 drops yellow food-gel colouring
pink: 3 drops pink food-gel colouring
peach: 3 drops pink food-gel colouring and 3 drops orange food-gel colouring
purple: 3 drops purple food-gel colouring and 2 drops pink food-gel colouring
2 Rice Krispie bars

CAKE

2 batches Chocolate cake (page 41)

Fit the end of a piping bag with a small round tip and fill it with the white frosting. Pipe random little dots all over your cactus. To make the smaller cactus, repeat the same process with a Rice Krispie ball about the size of a plum.

For the purple spikey cactus, fit the end of a piping bag with a small leaf tip and fill it with the purple frosting. Begin by piping a circle of leaves onto the baking paper, about 5 cm (2 in) in diameter, then fill that in with more leaves. As you pull away from the bottom, try and pull the piping bag straight up to give the leaves some height. If you feel it needs more volume, pipe some extra smaller leaves on top.

For the pickle cactus, pipe some tall pickle shapes about 5 cm (2 in) in height with the lime-green frosting. Do it slowly so that you don't risk them toppling over. Pipe a little bulb of pink frosting on top using a small round tip.

For the spikey bulb cactus, fit a piping bag with a Wilton 8B tip and fill it with the teal frosting. Pipe some frilly looking bulbs onto the baking paper, then pipe some little peach flowers on top using a small, closed-star tip and the peach buttercream. To finish, pipe little white buttercream spikes all over the cactus.

These are just some of the cacti I have made, but I'd encourage you guys to hop online and look at the thousands of cacti designs. Be inspired and experiment with your own designs and colour combinations. Once you've finished making your cacti, pop them in the fridge for at least 2 hours to chill.

CAKE

For this recipe, you'll need to make two batches of the chocolate cake. Bake, then allow to cool.

TO DECORATE

Crumb-coat the cake using the raspberry frosting (see page 10). To prepare the striped frosting, add the peach and white frosting to two separate piping bags.

Pipe a ring of peach frosting around the bottom of your cake, then a ring of white frosting above that. Repeat until you get to the top of the cake. Add some more peach frosting to the top. Use a small offset spatula to spread it out, aiming to get it flat. It doesn't have to be perfect, because we're going to come back to it.

Use a cake scraper (see page 26) to carefully scrape the frosting around the cake. Scrape any excess frosting off the cake scraper each time you go around the cake to ensure the different layers of coloured frosting stay nice and neat. Continue scraping until the cake is smooth on the sides, then gently smooth out the top with the scraper.

Fill a piping bag with the teal ganache and drizzle it around the top of the cake, letting it drip down the side.

Finish by carefully adding the chilled cacti decorations to the top.

See image on page 100.

CACTUS GARDEN *cake*

MAGIC MUSHROOM *cake*

MAGIC MUSHROOM *cake*

HARD

SERVES **30**

MAGIC MUSHROOMS

1 batch American buttercream frosting (page 45)
1 tablespoon unsweetened (Dutch) cocoa powder
5 drops red food-gel colouring

CHOCOLATE BARK

500 g (1 lb 2 oz) dark chocolate, melted
300 g (10½ oz) white chocolate and 100 g (3½ oz) dark chocolate, melted together

CAKE

2 batches Chocolate cake (page 41)
300 g (10½ oz) mint slice cookies, chopped

GRASS FROSTING

1 batch American buttercream frosting (page 45)
light-green: 4 drops green food-gel colouring
green: 4 drops green food-gel colouring and 2 drops blue food-gel colouring
dark-green: 4 drops green food-gel colouring, 2 drops blue food-gel colouring and 3 drops purple food-gel colouring

FROSTING

2 batches Chocolate ganache (page 49)
1 batch chocolate-flavoured Swiss meringue buttercream frosting (page 46)

There was this song back in kindergarten that scared the crap out of me. Every time we'd sing it, I would get the shivers and get so terrified I'd start crying. It was called 'We're Going On A Bear Hunt'. The idea of going into a deep, dark forest where anything could eat you, like a huge bear, still scares me. The bears can stay in the forest and I'm happy out of it. This cake kind of gives me the shivers, because even as an adult, I'm still not sure if fairies are actually good or not. But look how pretty it is! It's inspired by a magic forest and magic mushrooms – the delicious kind, not the kind that make you giggle at your hands.

MAGIC MUSHROOMS

To make the magic mushrooms, set aside 2 tablespoons of plain frosting in a small bowl. Add the cocoa powder to the remaining frosting and mix until well combined. Divide the cocoa-flavoured frosting in half and add the red food gel to one half. Mix until evenly coloured.

Fit the end of a piping bag with a large, round tip and fill it with the light cocoa frosting. Pipe ten long upright stalks onto a baking tray lined with baking paper. Chill.

Fit the end of another piping bag with a large, round tip and fill it with the red frosting. Pipe ten low, wide bulbs onto the baking paper. Add little blobs of white frosting to create the white-spot details on the mushrooms. Chill the stalks and mushroom heads for about 40 minutes to get them nice and cold.

Once the stalks are chilled, use a very sharp knife to cut off the very top, creating an even, flat surface. Add a little dab of frosting to the top of the stalk and stick the mushroom head on top. Stand them up on a baking tray lined with baking paper and chill until ready to use.

CHOCOLATE BARK

Lay a long piece of baking paper on a flat work surface. Drizzle the melted dark chocolate on top and use a large offset spatula to spread it out. Leave to set completely. Use a fork to add some grooves in the set chocolate before you drizzle some light chocolate randomly on top. Use the back of a tablespoon to spread it around. Let that second layer set completely before using a sharp knife dipped in boiling water to cut the bark into different shapes and shards – kind of like random-sized pieces of wood flooring.

FLOWERS

- ¼ batch American buttercream frosting (page 45)
- 2 drops blue food-gel colouring
- 2 drops pink food-gel colouring
- 2 drops yellow food-gel colouring
- 2 drops orange food-gel colouring

CAKE

Make, bake and chill the chocolate cakes. To trim the cakes, see page 10.

When filling the cake, pipe chocolate ganache in between each layer and add some chopped mint cookies before topping with the next cake layer. Crumb-coat the cake (see page 10) using the ganache, then chill.

GRASS FROSTING

Divide the frosting between three bowls. Use the colour formulations in the ingredients list to colour the frosting three different shades of green.

Fit the end of a piping bag with a grass tip. Using a tablespoon to transfer the frosting, line one side of your bag with the dark green frosting. Line the other side with the green frosting and fill the centre of the piping bag with the light-green frosting

FLOWERS

Divide the frosting between four bowls. Use the colour formulations in the ingredients list to colour the frosting blue, pink, yellow and orange. Fit the end of three piping bags with Wilton #4 tips and fill with the blue, yellow and orange frostings. For the pink flowers, fit the end of a piping bag with a small star tip and fill with the pink frosting.

TO DECORATE

Add a layer of chocolate-flavoured Swiss meringue buttercream as the final layer of frosting (see page 12) to the cake, then carefully transfer the cake onto its cake stand. Stick the chocolate bark around the side of the cake.

Pipe grass frosting on top of the cake and around the bottom, onto the cake stand, then use the blue, yellow and orange flower frostings to pipe random mini flower blobs of each colour in the grass. Next, create more flowers in the grass using the pink frosting. Top these pink flowers with a tiny blob of yellow frosting to create the stamen.

To finish, add the buttercream mushrooms.

See image on page 101.

MEDIUM

MAKES **30** SANDWICHED MACARONS

MACARONS

1 batch Vanilla macarons (page 42)
1 teaspoon bubblegum flavouring
4 drops pink food-gel colouring

FROSTING

1 teaspoon bubblegum flavouring
3 drops blue food-gel colouring
1 batch Swiss meringue buttercream frosting (page 46)

DECORATIONS

95 g (3¼ oz/½ cup) rainbow caviar sprinkles
½ batch Vanilla cake (page 37) or use a 20 cm (8 in) store-bought cake, sliced into 1 cm (½ in) slices

Guys! These were the first macarons I made on The Scran Line, and they're still some of my fave macarons, and yours! They're just so cute and bubblegum pop, it makes me sick! Speaking of bubblegum, these are bubblegum-flavoured, but you can pretty much flavour them with any food flavouring you like.

MACARONS

When making the meringue for the macarons, add the bubblegum flavouring and pink food gel at about the 3-minute mark.

Once the macarons have been piped, sprinkle with the rainbow caviar sprinkles. Allow to dry before baking.

FROSTING

Add the bubblegum flavouring and blue food gel to the frosting and mix until well combined.

ASSEMBLY

To assemble the macarons, use the wide end of a piping tip – about 1 cm/½ in in diameter – to cut out small rounds of vanilla cake.

Fit the end of a piping bag with a Wilton #32 tip and fill with the frosting. Pipe small rings of frosting on the flat side of half the macaron shells. Fill the centre of the frosting rings with the rounds of cake and sandwich with the remaining shells.

FORBIDDEN DOUGHNUT macarons

MEDIUM

MAKES **15** SANDWICHED MACARONS

INSPIRED BY: ***THE SIMPSONS***

Mmmmm ... Doughnuts ... ARGHHHHH! I don't think you guys know this about me, but I used to want to be a cartoonist when I was a kid. In fact, I developed a character named Granooligan who loved to cross-dress and had a bit of a cheeky side to him. Of course, now I know, deep down, he was a drag queen. Anyhoo ... Matt Groening, the creator of *The Simpsons*, is a hero of mine because I absolutely love *The Simpsons*. It's really special to me, and I wanted to pay homage to it with this macaron. Because I, like Homer, love doughnuts!

ROYAL ICING

250 g (9 oz) icing (confectioners') sugar
2½ tablespoons powdered egg whites
1 drop pink food-gel colouring
1 teaspoon vanilla extract or strawberry flavouring

FROSTING

2 teaspoons ground cinnamon
1 batch American buttercream frosting (page 45)

MACARON SHELLS

1 batch Vanilla macarons (page 42)
1 tablespoon unsweetened (Dutch) cocoa powder
4 drops yellow food-gel colouring
250 g (9 oz) rainbow jimmies

ROYAL ICING

You can make this icing in a stand mixer fitted with the paddle attachment, or you can use a hand mixer.

Combine the icing sugar and powdered egg whites in a large mixing bowl. Once the two ingredients are well combined, add 1 tablespoon water, the pink food gel and the vanilla, then mix until well combined. The consistency you're looking for is a mixture thin enough to pipe, but stiff enough to hold its shape and not be a runny mess. If your mixture is too stiff, add a little more water, 1 teaspoon at a time, until you reach the right consistency.

FROSTING

Add the cinnamon to the buttercream and mix until well combined.

MACARON SHELLS

When making the macaron batter, add the cocoa powder with the icing sugar and almond flour.

Add the yellow food gel at about the 3-minute mark.

To pipe the bottom shells, fill a piping bag fitted with a medium round tip with the macaron batter and pipe rounds of batter, about 3.5 cm (1½ in) in diameter, onto your prepared trays. Make sure you space them 2 cm (¾ in) apart.

For the top shells, you want to create doughnut-like shapes. A good way to get a consistent doughnut shape is to dip a 3 cm (1½ in) round cookie cutter into the macaron batter, then 'stamp' rounds onto your baking trays. Pipe a ring of macaron batter following the outline of each circle to create the doughnut 'tops'.

Once they're all piped, leave the macaron shells to rest before you bake them.

ASSEMBLY

To decorate the macarons, fit the end of a piping bag with a very small round tip. Fill with royal icing and pipe a zig-zag on top of

a doughnut-shaped shell, around its outer edge, followed by a circle around the inner edge of the doughnut shell. Next, fill the shape in with more icing. Filling in your shape is called 'flooding'. Once all of your top shells are flooded, gently shake them from side to side. This will help smooth out the icing and fill in any gaps. Sprinkle with rainbow jimmies. Once decorated, leave the shells to set at room temperature for 2 hours.

Fit a piping bag with a medium round tip, fill it with cinnamon frosting and pipe a ring of frosting on the flat side of the bottom shells. Sandwich with the top shells.

MEDIUM

MAKES **30** SANDWICHED MACARONS

PEACH JELLY

200 g (7 oz) tinned peaches, drained
3 teaspoons powdered gelatin

FROSTING

2 drops pink food-gel colouring
2 drops orange food-gel colouring
1 teaspoon peach flavouring (see Note)
1 batch American buttercream frosting (page 45)

MACARONS

1 batch Vanilla macarons (page 42)
2 drops pink food-gel colouring
1 teaspoon peach flavouring
1 can orange Color Mist food colouring spray
1 can pink Color Mist food colouring spray

Note
I bought this peach flavouring online. You can find so many conventional and unconventional flavours online – the possibilities are endless.

Is there anything more gorgeous than the colour peach? I mean, my fave colour is mint, but I used a gorgeous golden peach colour on the back of these macarons when I photographed them and it is, to this day, the most popular photo I've posted on Instagram. That's not the only gorgeous thing about these macarons; they're filled with a delicious peach jelly too.

PEACH JELLY

Line a 20 × 20 cm (8 × 8 in) baking tin with plastic wrap. Set aside.

Add the peaches to a food processor or blender and process to a smooth purée. Set aside.

Put 3 tablespoons cold water in a small bowl, sprinkle the gelatin on top and mix until well combined. Leave to set for 5 minutes, then microwave on high for 10 seconds to melt it. Pour it into the peach purée and mix well.

Pour the peach mixture into the baking tin and refrigerate for 3 hours. Once it has set, use the wide end of a small metal piping tip (about 1 cm/½ in) to cut out peach jelly discs for filling the macarons.

FROSTING

Add the food gels and peach flavouring to the frosting and mix until well combined.

MACARONS

When making the meringue for the macarons, add the pink food gel and peach flavouring at about the 3-minute mark. Scrape down the side of the bowl at least once to ensure the meringue is evenly coloured.

To add a second layer of colour to your macarons, place a row of eight baked shells on a sheet of baking paper, round side up. Spray one half of each shell with orange Color Mist, and the other half with pink Color Mist. Leave them to dry for 10 minutes. Don't spray too closely or too heavily – hold the can about 10 cm (4 in) away from the shells. Repeat until all the shells have been sprayed.

ASSEMBLY

Fit the end of a piping bag with a Wilton #32 tip, fill with the frosting and pipe a ring of frosting on the flat side of half the macarons, leaving a hole in the centre. Place a peach jelly disc in each hole, then sandwich with the remaining shells.

EASY

MAKES 30 SANDWICHED MACARONS

MACARONS

1 batch Vanilla macarons (page 42)
2 tablespoons unsweetened (Dutch) cocoa powder, sifted
12 drops black food-gel colouring
3 tablespoons pink sea salt flakes (optional)

SAUCE

3 teaspoons Vegemite
½ batch Salted caramel sauce (page 50)

FROSTING

1–2 teaspoons Vegemite
½ batch American buttercream frosting (page 45)

You know what really annoys me? When I see videos of unsuspecting Americans being told to try and eat an entire spoon of Vegemite. Half of them expect it to be sweet. It's not! Aussies grow up on the tangy-salty spread and we love it. Here's how to wrap your head around a Vegemite macaron: you know how salted caramel is loads better than regular, overly sweet caramel? Well, we're just making it a little saltier with the addition of Vegemite. I stand by these macarons. They're weird, but in the most delicious way.

MACARONS

When making the macaron batter, add the cocoa powder with the almond flour and icing sugar.

Add the black food gel to the meringue at about the 3-minute mark. Scrape down the side of the bowl at least once to ensure the meringue is evenly coloured.

Once the macarons have been piped and had time to dry, sprinkle with the sea salt flakes, if using.

SAUCE

Add the Vegemite to the salted caramel sauce and mix until well combined. Transfer to a squeeze bottle.

FROSTING

Add the Vegemite to the frosting and mix until well combined.

ASSEMBLY

To assemble the macarons, fit the end of a piping bag with a Wilton 6B tip, fill with the frosting and pipe a ring of frosting on the flat side of half the macaron shells. Fill the holes with salted caramel sauce and top with the remaining shells.

REBEL FREAK SHOW

When I was little, we lived in a neighbourhood where there were a lot of kids my age. The girl who lived a couple of houses down the road from us was named Amber. Her mum was American.

The only time we'd see Amber was at Halloween when she'd go around trick-or-treating in a neighbourhood where nobody celebrated Halloween. It's not really big in Australia, but that poor kid persevered. She'd get dressed in her costume and go around knocking on people's houses asking for treats. She would knock on our door, but my mum was so dead against Halloween that she wouldn't even open it.

I was always jealous of her because you'd see how much fun Halloween was in movies and TV shows. You get to dress up in a costume: fun, and you get free sweets: yum.

What's not to love?

Now that I'm an adult, besides being allowed to stay up as late as I want, I get to celebrate Halloween with you guys through macarons, cupcakes and cakes, OH MY! I love all the typical Halloween stuff, like monsters and witches, but I like to put my own twist on things when it comes to my Halloween treats.

For example, Gaga's vampire-queen character in *American Horror Story* is what inspired my Vampire kiss cupcakes (see www.thescranline.com) – they're glossy, sexy and elegant. My Good witch, bad bish cupcakes (page 116) were inspired by the drag outfit Todrick Hall wore in his song 'Low'. (YouTube that music video – it's brilliant.) Fun fact: a follower of mine showed him that cupcake and he loved it!

EASY

MAKES **20** CUPCAKES

INSPIRED BY: ***THE SIMPSONS***

20 white cupcake cases

BRAIN WORMS

straight plastic drinking straws
5 teaspoons powdered gelatin
4 packets green jelly (jello)
1 drop yellow food-gel colouring

CUPCAKES

1 batch Vanilla cupcakes (page 34)
2 drops leaf green food-gel colouring

DECORATIONS

250 ml (8½ fl oz/1 cup) Chocolate sauce (page 51)
2 drops black food-gel colouring
2 tablespoons silver lustre dust
1 teaspoon vodka or vanilla extract

FROSTING

2 drops black food-gel colouring (add more if you want it darker)
1 batch chocolate-flavoured American buttercream frosting (page 45)

Superfoods move over; brain food is here. These cupcakes will regenerate any brain during Halloween, and they have real-life (but not really) brain worms that move. (Except they definitely don't move ...)

BRAIN WORMS

Tightly pack drinking straws into a tall glass, the taller the better.

Combine the gelatin and 1 tablespoon cold water in a bowl and set aside for 5 minutes.

Follow the instructions on the box to prepare the jelly. I'd recommend using half the amount of boiling water suggested to make the worms firmer.

Add the gelatin mixture and yellow food gel to the jelly and mix until completely melted.

Slowly pour the liquid jelly into the drinking straws, then refrigerate for a couple of hours, or until completely set. Overnight is best.

CUPCAKES & DECORATIONS

When making the cupcake batter, add the green food gel with the wet ingredients. Bake, then allow to cool.

To prepare the chocolate sauce, add the black food gel and mix well. Transfer to a squeeze bottle and set aside.

To prepare the silver paint, combine the lustre dust and vodka in a small bowl and mix well. Set aside.

FROSTING

Combine the black food gel with the frosting and mix until well combined.

ASSEMBLY

Core the centre of each cupcake with an apple corer (stop about 1 cm (½ in) from the bottom) and fill with the black chocolate sauce, reserving some to top the cupcakes.

Fit the end of a piping bag with a large, round tip, fill with the frosting and pipe each cupcake in a double-doughnut swirl (see page 14). Chill the cupcakes for 30 minutes.

Use a toothpick to create stitch patterns in the firm frosting. Gently paint over the pattern with the silver paint and allow to dry for 5 minutes.

Once the worms have set, squeeze them out of the straws. If they won't come out, place the glass holding the straws into a bowl of warm water for 30 seconds. That should soften the jelly so that the worms come out easily. (You want to transfer the jelly worms straight to the cupcakes when they're ready to decorate, because putting them all in a bowl will cause them to stick together and then break apart when you try to disentangle them.)

Finish by squeezing some remaining black chocolate sauce over the frosting and piling the brain worms on top.

GOOD WITCH, BAD BISH *cupcakes*

HARD

MAKES **15** CUPCAKES

INSPIRED BY: **LOW – TODRICK HALL**

15 white cupcake cases

FROSTING

2 drops green food-gel colouring
1 batch Swiss meringue buttercream frosting (page 46)

GANACHE

150 g (5½ oz) white chocolate buttons
100 ml (3½ fl oz) thickened (whipping) cream

CANDY SHARDS

black: 100 g (3½ oz) Wilton black candy melts, melted
green: 100 g (3½ oz) Wilton green candy melts, melted
pink: 100 g (3½ oz) Wilton pink candy melts, melted and 100 g (3½ oz) Wilton white candy melts, melted
blue: 100 g (3½ oz) Wilton blue candy melts, melted and 100 g (3½ oz) Wilton white candy melts, melted
100 g (3½ oz) pearl lustre dust, for dusting

CUPCAKES

1 batch Vanilla cupcakes (page 34)

TO COLOUR THE DARK SIDE
black: 1 tablespoon food-safe activated charcoal or 1 tablespoon unsweetened (Dutch) cocoa powder and 4 drops black food-gel colouring
blue: 5 drops royal blue food-gel colouring and 2 drops purple food-gel colouring
green: 3 drops green food-gel colouring

I would like you to stop what you're doing, hop on YouTube and look up Todrick Hall, 'Low'. It's an amazing song, but the best thing about that song is the outfits and costumes that Ru Paul and Todrick wear in the music video. That is what these cupcakes are inspired by. I just love everything about Todrick Hall. He's so talented, he exudes so much confidence and I feel really inspired by that.

FROSTING

Add the green food gel to the buttercream and mix until well combined.

GANACHE

Combine the white chocolate and cream in a large, microwave-safe bowl. Microwave on high, for 20 seconds at a time, mixing well between each interval. Cover with plastic wrap and leave to set.

CANDY SHARDS

Melt all the different candy melts separately, then mix the various colours together according to the colour formulations in the ingredients list.

Line four baking trays with baking paper. Pour the melted candies onto separate baking trays. Spread out using a cake scraper or ruler to get nice thin, even layers.

Leave to set for about 4 minutes, then use a large, warm knife to gently score the candy into diamond shapes about the size of a fingernail. Dust each shard with the pearl lustre dust.

CUPCAKES & ASSEMBLY

Once the cake batter is ready, divide it between six mixing bowls. Add the charcoal powder to one and mix until well combined. Colour the rest blue, green, pink, light blue and white. Transfer the coloured batters to separate piping bags.

To create the illusion that one half of the cupcake is a good witch and the other is a bad bish, you'll need to pipe the colours in layers. I'm not going to lie – this part of the recipe is very time consuming. Throw on your fave album or podcast and get piping.

Start off by piping black batter on the left side of each cupcake case. Pipe pink batter on the right side. Pipe little squiggles of green and blue batter on top of the black batter, and light blue and white on the pink batter. Pipe another layer of black batter on top of the blue and green squiggles, and another layer of pink batter on top of the light blue and white squiggles. Repeat until you've filled the cases three-quarters of the way. Bake, then allow to cool.

TO COLOUR THE LIGHT SIDE
pink: ½ drop deep pink food-gel colouring
light blue: ½ drop sky blue food-gel colouring
white: 4 drops white food-gel colouring

Core the centre of each cupcake with an apple corer (stop about 1 cm (½ in) from the bottom) and fill with chocolate ganache.

Fit the end of a piping bag with a round tip, fill with the green frosting and pipe a swirl of frosting on top of each cupcake. You can make these as high or as low as you like.

Stick the black and green shards on the right side of the frosting, over the 'bad bish' side, and attach the pink and blue shards on the left side of the frosting.

EASY

MAKES **20** CUPCAKES

20 brown cupcake cases

CUPCAKES

1 batch Red velvet cupcakes (page 33)
4 drops black food-gel colouring

FROSTING

1 batch chocolate-flavoured American buttercream frosting (page 45)
3 drops black food-gel colouring

BLOOD SYRUP

140 g (5 oz) red sour straps (about 15), or red liquorice
125 ml (4 fl oz/½ cup) corn syrup (or maple syrup, golden syrup or simple syrup – any syrup will do)
1 drop liquid red food dye

DECORATIONS

15 g (½ oz/½ cup) Rice Krispies
125 ml (4 fl oz/½ cup) corn syrup (or maple syrup, golden syrup or simple syrup – any syrup will do)
140 g (5 oz) red sour straps (about 15), or red liquorice

Dead velvet cupcakes with Rice Krispie maggots and edible blood and guts are sure to impress anyone, or gross them out. Either way, these cupcakes make an impression and they're a lot of fun to make!

CUPCAKES

When making the cupcakes, replace the red food dye in the red velvet recipe with black food gel. Add the food gel with the wet ingredients. Bake, then allow to cool.

FROSTING

To prepare the frosting, add the food gel to the buttercream and mix until well combined.

BLOOD & GUTS

Prepare your blood and guts by splitting the sour straps into separate long strips. You can do this by hand or using a knife.

Prepare the blood syrup by gently combining the corn syrup and red food dye in a large mixing bowl. Add the sour straps and mix well.

ASSEMBLY

Core the centre of each cupcake with an apple corer (stop about 1 cm (½ in) from the bottom) and fill it with the blood and guts mixture.

Fit the end of a piping bag with a medium round tip, fill with the frosting and pipe a swirl of frosting on top of each cupcake. Use a blunt knife to make claw marks in the frosting as if a wolverine has tried to pick it up. Add your Rice Krispie maggots around the frosting and finish off with a drizzle of blood syrup.

EASY

MAKES **20** CUPCAKES

INSPIRED BY: **FASHION! – LADY GAGA FT. RUPAUL**

20 black cupcake cases

CUPCAKES

1 batch Red velvet cupcakes (page 33)
5 drops black food-gel colouring

FROSTING

8 drops black food-gel colouring
1 batch chocolate-flavoured American buttercream frosting (page 45)

CANDY SPIKES

400 g (14 oz) Wilton black candy melts, melted

YouTube: Gaga, RuPaul 'Fashion!'. When I first discovered this clip, I could not stop watching it. I was obsessed and still am, it's so iconic. I just love everything about it and I really look up to these two amazing artists. There's a lyric in the song that they added just for that performance: 'Chic. Freak. Slay.' I love it. It's what inspired these cupcakes.

CUPCAKES

When making the cupcake batter, replace the red food dye with the black food gel. Bake, then allow to cool.

FROSTING

Add the black food gel to the frosting and mix until well combined.

CANDY SPIKES

To make the candy spikes, spread the melted candy onto a baking tray lined with baking paper. Allow to set.

Dip a sharp knife in hot water and dry it off. Carefully cut the candy into spikes, then set aside.

ASSEMBLY

Fit the end of a piping bag with a medium round tip, fill with the frosting and pipe a narrow, tall swirl of frosting on top of each cupcake. Stick the spikes to the frosting, starting at the top and working your way down.

SILICONE DAYDREAM cupcakes

HARD

MAKES **20** CUPCAKES

INSPIRED BY: **DANCE IN THE DARK – LADY GAGA**

20 white cupcake cases

CUPCAKES

1 batch Vanilla cupcakes (page 34)

BLOOD SYRUP

2 tablespoons corn syrup
1 teaspoon liquid red food dye

FROSTING

2 drops pink food-gel colouring
2 drops red food-gel colouring
1 teaspoon mango flavouring
1 batch Swiss meringue buttercream frosting (page 46)

SKIN MIRROR GLAZE

20 g (¾ oz) powdered gelatin
200 ml (7 fl oz) sweetened condensed milk
300 g (10½ oz) granulated sugar
350 g (12½ oz) white chocolate chips
½ drop pink food-gel colouring
½ drop orange food-gel colouring

No jokes – for this cupcake, you're going to be performing surgery. Not on anything that's alive though.

CUPCAKES

Bake the vanilla cupcakes, then allow to cool.

BLOOD SYRUP

To make the blood syrup, combine the corn syrup and red food dye in a mixing bowl. Set aside.

FROSTING

Line a baking tray with baking paper.

Add the food gels and mango flavouring to the frosting and mix until well combined.

Fit the end of a piping bag with a medium round tip, fill with the frosting and pipe 20 cupcake-sized swirls onto the baking paper. Refrigerate for 2 hours.

SKIN MIRROR GLAZE

Combine the gelatin and 125 ml (4 fl oz/½ cup) water in a small mixing bowl and set aside for 5 minutes.

Heat the milk, sugar and 150 ml (5 fl oz) water in a saucepan over a medium heat and bring to a simmer. Add the bloomed gelatin and stir until dissolved.

Place the white chocolate in a large, heatproof bowl. Pour the hot milk mixture over the chocolate and let it sit for 5 minutes. Once the chocolate has softened, add the food gels. Use a hand-held blender (or a hand whisk) to smooth out the mixture, then pass it through a fine-mesh sieve to remove any remaining lumps. Pour the glaze into a pouring jug.

ASSEMBLY

Turn a narrow drinking glass upside down and place a frosting swirl on top. Pour the mirror glaze over the swirl. Repeat with the remaining swirls, using a small offset spatula to transfer the glazed swirls to a lined baking tray. Refrigerate for 1 hour until set. If the mirror glaze is going on too thin and is translucent, let it cool down a little more before using.

Once chilled, carefully transfer each glazed swirl to a cupcake using the spatula and a fork to help slide the frosting off the spatula.

Use a scalpel to cut out a tiny wedge of the mirror glaze to expose the frosting underneath, then dip a toothpick into the blood syrup and drizzle some on the bottom of the incision.

VOODOO HALLOWEEN *cake*

MEDIUM

SERVES **30**

INSPIRED BY: **MONSTER – LADY GAGA**

CHOCOLATE SKULL

1.6 kg (3½ lb) dark cooking chocolate buttons
3 tablespoons food-safe activated charcoal

CAKE

2 batches Chocolate cake (page 41)
10 drops black food-gel colouring
2 teaspoons blackberry flavouring
3 bubble straws or plastic dowel rods

WHITE FROSTING

2 batches Swiss meringue buttercream frosting (page 46)

BLACK FROSTING

40 g (1½ oz) food-safe activated charcoal
2 batches chocolate-flavoured Swiss meringue buttercream frosting (page 46)

DECORATIONS

1 batch Chocolate sauce (page 51)

GOLD PAINT

40 g (1½ oz) gold lustre dust
160 ml (5½ fl oz) vodka or vanilla extract

Mirror, mirror on the wall, who's the fiercest of them all? Face, face, face, body and all.

CHOCOLATE SKULL

To make the chocolate skull, you'll need a skull mould about half the size of a real adult skull. I bought mine online, but if you're making this around Halloween time, you'll be able to find them at cake decorating stores.

To colour the chocolate, melt it in the microwave on high, for 20 seconds at a time, mixing well between each interval. It's a lot of chocolate, so it may take a while to melt.

Once completely melted and smooth, add the charcoal and mix until evenly coloured.

Fill the skull mould with the chocolate and chill overnight.

CAKE

When making the cake batter, add the black food gel and blackberry flavouring with the wet ingredients. Bake, then allow to cool.

Use the white frosting to fill and crumb-coat the cake (see page 10).

Next, prepare your cake supports. They will stop the heavy chocolate skull from sinking into the cake. You can use bubble straws or plastic dowel rods, available at your local cake supply store or online. You will need three straws.

Insert one bubble straw into the cake. When it hits the bottom, lift it out and use a food-safe marker to mark where the straw needs to be cut to sit level with the surface of the cake. Use the straw as a guide to cut the other straws. Push all straws into the cake. Top with a 15 cm (6 in) cake board. Cover the cake board with more white frosting and spread it out evenly using a small offset spatula. Chill for 2 hours.

TO DECORATE

To prepare the black frosting, add the charcoal to the chocolate frosting and mix until well combined. To frost the cake, see page 12.

Drizzle the top of the cake with chocolate sauce and let it drip down the side. Carefully place the skull on top, sitting on its side, positioned over the cake board. Chill for 4 hours, or overnight.

Combine the gold lustre dust and vodka in a mixing bowl and mix until well combined.

Use a small, food-safe paintbrush to paint the chocolate drizzle and skull with gold paint. You may need to do two coats of gold.

HARD

MAKES **30** SANDWICHED MACARONS

INSPIRED BY: **MALEFICENT FROM *SLEEPING BEAUTY***

MACARONS

1 batch Vanilla macarons (page 42)
2 drops pink food-gel colouring
2 drops yellow food-gel colouring
1 teaspoon strawberry flavouring

DECORATIONS

2 teaspoons silver-star sprinkles
1 can purple Color Mist food colouring spray
1 can purple black Color Mist food colouring spray

FROSTING

2 drops blue food-gel colouring
2 teaspoons blackberry flavouring
1 batch Swiss meringue buttercream frosting (page 46)

Witches Bishes! These Halloween-themed macarons are inspired by the OG evil queen Maleficent from *Sleeping Beauty*. They directly reflect her dark soul as she peers into a gorgeous gold-rimmed mirror asking it who is the fairest of them all.

MACARONS

When making the meringue, add the food gels and strawberry flavouring at about the 3-minute mark.

Once the macarons have been piped and you've tapped each tray, sprinkle the shells with silver-star sprinkles.

To decorate, line up about eight macaron shells at a time on a large piece of baking paper. Spray with the purple mist to come about halfway up the shells, then spray the black mist just on the very tip of the shells on the purple side to create a gradient effect. Allow to dry.

FROSTING

To prepare the frosting, add the blue food gel and blackberry flavouring to the buttercream and mix until well combined.

ASSEMBLY

Fit the end of a piping bag with a Wilton 6B tip, fill with the frosting and pipe a swirl of frosting on the flat side of half the macaron shells. Sandwich with the remaining shells.

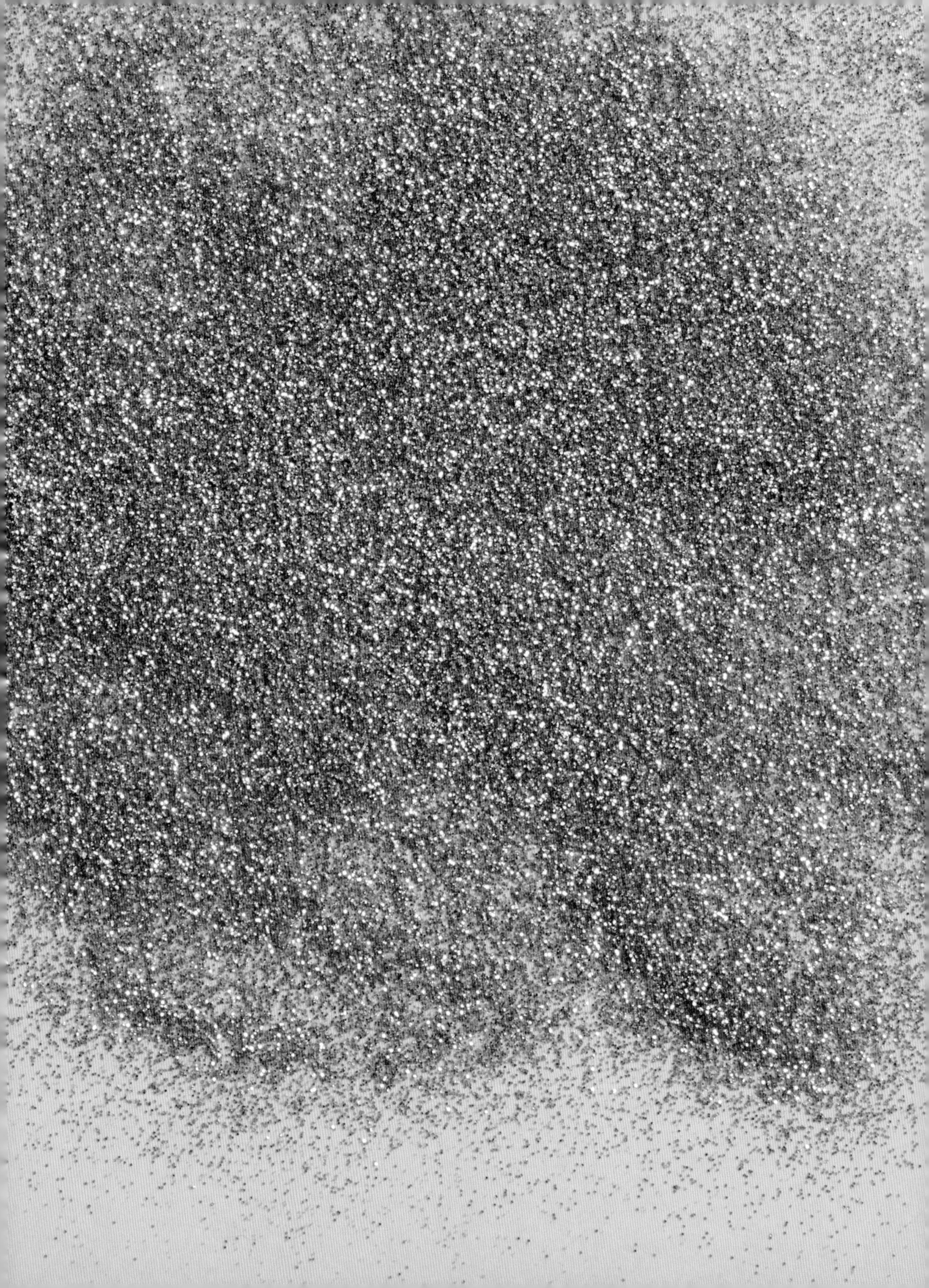

REBEL THIRST QUENCHERS

Is there anything more gorgeous than a thick strawberry or choc-mint milkshake with a pile of frilly whipped cream and sprinkles on top?

Yes. The answer is yes. It's this collection of cupcakes.

Oh, also, this collection of cupcakes is the most commonly drawn of all my desserts. No idea why, but you guys love drawing these cupcakes! If you ever draw one of my desserts, tag me on Instagram (@thescranline).

MINT CHOC-CHIP FREAKSHAKE *cupcakes*

MEDIUM

MAKES **10** CUPCAKES

10 white cupcake cases

CUPCAKES & DOUGHNUTS

1 batch Vanilla cupcakes (page 34)
2 drops leaf green food-gel colouring
2 drops sky blue food-gel colouring
1 teaspoon peppermint extract
250 g (9 oz) mini dark chocolate chips

FROSTING

½ batch Chocolate ganache frosting (page 49)

DECORATIONS

400 ml (13½ fl oz) Chocolate sauce (page 51)
200 g (7 oz) crushed mints
10 mint-chocolate ball candies
200 g (7 oz) pink fairy floss (cotton candy)
20 mini paper straws, to decorate (optional)

I get a tweet from Yolanda Gampp one day saying: 'Hey Nick, let's collab.' So, naturally, I pee myself a little from excitement and then reply, 'Yes!'

First thing I do is start sketching. That's the first step for all my desserts. Yo's fave flavour is mint choc-chip, so I knew it had to be that flavour. This particular cupcake was all about freakshakes, which were trending at the time. Once it was sketched, I sent the design to Yo. She loved it.

The next step was to bake it and test it out. Now, when I sketch my desserts, more often than not they come out looking exactly the same as the sketch on the first try, with some minor adjustments. I know! I'm still just as surprised as you are that that actually happens. This particular cupcake looked nothing like the original sketch. It was a disaster on the first try, but I had all the elements there in front of me, so I played around with some different shapes and styles and it turned out absolutely amazing in the end. Yo loved it, she caked it, 'cos, you know, that's what Yo does. And here we are today: the most viewed video on my channel and the most iconic Scran Line cupcake next to the Bubblepop electric cupcake (page 56).

CUPCAKES & DOUGHNUTS

Line a cupcake tin with the cupcake cases. Spray a doughnut tin with oil and use a paper towel to wipe away any excess. Set aside.

When making the cupcake batter, add the food gels and peppermint extract with the wet ingredients.

Once the batter is ready, fold in the mini chocolate chips using a spatula.

Transfer the batter to a piping bag and snip off the end, ensuring that the hole is big enough to allow the chocolate chips through.

Pipe the batter into the doughnut baking tin, filling the moulds halfway. Give the tin a gentle tap to help any air bubbles at the bottom rise to the top.

Fill each cupcake case three-quarters of the way. Bake the doughnuts for 15 minutes and the cupcakes for 40 minutes. Allow the cupcakes to cool.

To get the doughnuts out of the hot doughnut tin, place a wire rack directly on top of the tin. Grip the tin and the rack with two tea towels (dish towels) and flip it over. Gently tap the base of the doughnut tin. This will allow the doughnuts to fall out easily without them tearing. It's best to do this as soon as they come out of the oven to stop them from cooking any further as the tin cools.

ASSEMBLY

Dip the top of each cupcake into the chocolate sauce, letting any excess drip off. Hold the cupcake on its side and sprinkle the top with crushed mint candy.

Core the centre of each cupcake with an apple corer (stop about 1 cm (½ in) from the bottom) and fill with chocolate sauce. Let the cupcakes sit for 10 minutes to allow the sauce to set a little before you start the frosting.

Fit the end of a piping bag with a large round tip, fill with chocolate ganache and frost your cupcakes in a double-doughnut swirl (see page 14).

Push a cake doughnut into the ganache, upright, and drizzle over some more chocolate sauce, allowing it to drip down the side of the cupcakes. Carefully drizzle some chocolate sauce on top of the doughnut as well.

To finish your cupcakes, place a choc-mint candy ball in front of the doughnut and add a tuft of fairy floss right before serving.

I also like to add little paper straws to the frosting to make it feel more like a freakshake.

Note
If it's a warm day, your frosting may not be firm enough to hold the doughnut. Try adding a paper straw behind your doughnut to stop it from tipping backwards, or secure the doughnut to the cake with a toothpick to help hold it in place. If you do use a toothpick, make sure your guests know there's a spear in the middle of their cupcake, otherwise there'll be trips to the emergency room!

See image on page 132.

MINT CHOC-CHIP FREAKSHAKE *cupcakes*

WATERMELON FREAKSHAKE *cupcakes*

MEDIUM

MAKES **10** CUPCAKES

10 white cupcake cases

GREEN GANACHE

100 g (3½ oz) Wilton green candy melts
100 g (3½ oz) Wilton lime candy melts
100 ml (3½ fl oz) thickened (whipping) cream

FROSTING

1 drop green food-gel colouring
2 teaspoons watermelon flavouring
1 batch American buttercream frosting (page 45)

CUPCAKES & DOUGHNUTS

1 batch Vanilla cupcakes (page 34)
2 teaspoons watermelon flavouring
3 drops pink food-gel colouring
3 drops red food-gel colouring
220 g (8 oz/1 cup) mini dark chocolate chips

DECORATIONS

100 g (3½ oz) pink fairy floss (cotton candy)
20 mini paper straws, to decorate (optional)

'Hey Nick, when are you going to make watermelon cupcakes?'

I get a lot of requests from you guys, which is awesome. You all have amazing ideas. This particular request popped up time and time again. My aim is to be original, and watermelon cupcakes had already been made every which way. For me, it can take a while to come up with an idea to reinvent an existing design. Usually, a lot of thought goes into it, but sometimes the solution just pops into my head. This particular time, the solution came to me really easily. Here's my take on a watermelon cupcake.

GREEN GANACHE

Combine the candy melts and cream in a large, microwave-safe bowl and microwave on high, for 20 seconds at a time, mixing between each interval until smooth. Cover with plastic wrap and leave to set at room temperature.

FROSTING

Add the green food gel and watermelon flavouring to the frosting and mix until well combined.

CUPCAKES & DOUGHNUTS

Line a cupcake tin with the cupcake cases. Spray a doughnut tin with oil and use a paper towel to wipe away any excess. Set aside.

When making the cupcake batter, add the watermelon flavouring and food gels with the wet ingredients.

Once the batter is ready, fold in the mini chocolate chips until well combined.

Transfer the batter to a piping bag and snip off the end, ensuring that the hole is big enough to allow the chocolate chips through.

Pipe the batter into the doughnut tin, filling the moulds halfway. Give the tin a gentle tap to help any air bubbles at the bottom rise to the top.

Fill each cupcake case three-quarters of the way. Bake the doughnuts for 15 minutes and the cupcakes for 40 minutes. Allow the cupcakes to cool.

To get the doughnuts out of the hot doughnut tin, place a wire rack directly on top of the tin. Grip the tin and the rack with two tea towels (dish towels) and flip it over. Gently tap the base of the doughnut tin. This will allow the doughnuts to fall out easily without them ripping. It's best to do this as soon as they come out of the oven to stop them from cooking any further as the tin cools.

ASSEMBLY

Core the centre of each cupcake with an apple corer (stop about 1 cm (½ in) from the bottom) and fill with green ganache.

Fit the end of a piping bag with a Wilton 6B tip, fill with the frosting and pipe a double-doughnut swirl (see page 14) on top. Drizzle the green ganache over the frosting and carefully push a cake doughnut into the top, in an upright position.

Drizzle a little more green ganache over the doughnut and finish with a generous tuft of fairy floss right before serving.

I also like to add little paper straws to the frosting to make it feel more like a freakshake.

Note
If it's a warm day, your frosting may not be firm enough to hold the doughnut. Try adding a paper straw behind your doughnut to stop it from tipping backwards, or secure the doughnut to the cake with a toothpick to help hold it in place. If you do use a toothpick, make sure your guests know there's a spear in the middle of their cupcake, otherwise there'll be trips to the emergency room!

See image on page 133.

SUGAR-FREE MINT MOCHA MILKSHAKE *cupcakes*

EASY

MAKES **10** CUPCAKES

10 white cupcake cases

SUGAR-FREE CHOCOLATE SAUCE

200 g (7 oz) sugar-free dark chocolate chips (they don't have to be cooking chocolate)
50 g (1¾ oz) coconut oil
50 g (1¾ oz) granulated stevia (see Note)
250 ml (8½ fl oz/1 cup) thickened (whipping) cream

SUGAR-FREE BUTTERCREAM FROSTING

500 g (1 lb 2 oz) unsalted butter, softened
1.2 kg (2 lb 10 oz) powdered stevia
1 teaspoon glucose-free vanilla extract
1 teaspoon glucose-free peppermint extract
2 drops glucose-free sky blue food-gel colouring
2 drops glucose-free green food-gel colouring

CUPCAKES

1 batch Chocolate cupcakes (page 38)
225 g (8 oz) granulated stevia
1 tablespoon instant coffee

DECORATIONS

100 g (3½ oz) sugar-free dark chocolate, shaved
24 mini paper straws, to decorate (optional)

Before we go into this recipe, I wanted to include something sugar-free in the book for those of us who can't have sugar. This is by no means a healthy alternative to a regular cupcake. Good, healthy cupcakes don't exist, which is why you'll never see me attempt them.

This recipe can be adapted to use any flavour you like: chocolate and raspberry, plain chocolate, chocolate and coffee. It is, in essence, my chocolate cupcake recipe, but with stevia instead of regular sugar. It still tastes just as good though!

SUGAR-FREE CHOCOLATE SAUCE

Add all the ingredients to a large, microwave-safe bowl and microwave on high, for 20 seconds at a time, mixing well between each interval until smooth. Once it has cooled, the chocolate sauce will set in the cake and on top, so don't freak out thinking it's going to drip all over your guests.

SUGAR-FREE BUTTERCREAM FROSTING

Use a stand mixer or a hand mixer to soften the butter in a large bowl. Mix for 5 minutes so that it gains some volume and turns pale in colour.

Stop the mixer and add half the powdered stevia. Continue mixing on low speed until most of it has been incorporated, then beat on high speed for 5 minutes. Once the stevia is completely incorporated, stop the mixer and add the remaining stevia, vanilla extract and peppermint extract. Mix on low speed until just combined, then increase the speed to high and beat for 5–6 minutes until the mixture turns pale in colour.

Set about 100 g (3½ oz) of the frosting aside. Add the food gels to the remaining frosting and mix until evenly coloured.

CUPCAKES

When making the cupcake batter, replace the sugar in the recipe with stevia and add the instant coffee with the wet ingredients. Bake, then allow to cool.

ASSEMBLY

Core the centre of the cupcakes with an apple corer (stop about 1 cm (½ in) from the bottom) and fill with chocolate sauce. Fit the end of two piping bags with Wilton 1M tips, fill one with the green frosting and the other with the white frosting. Pipe a low swirl of green frosting on top of each cupcake. Drizzle with chocolate sauce and add a swirl of white frosting on top. Finish with a scattering of shaved sugar-free chocolate.

I also like to add little paper straws to the frosting to make it feel more like a milkshake.

Note

Stevia, or xylitol, is a natural sugar alternative that is suitable for people on a diabetic diet. If you can't find it in your local health-food store, a simple online search will bring up local websites that you can order it from. To make powdered stevia yourself, simply blitz granulated stevia in a food processor on high speed until it resembles a fine powder.

CHOC CHERRY COLA *cupcakes*

EASY

MAKES **10** CUPCAKES

INSPIRED BY: **CHERRY COLA – SAVAGE GARDEN**

OK, so if you've never heard of an Aussie band called Savage Garden, look them up on YouTube. They are absolute '90s Aussie gold. One of their songs, coincidently, is called 'Cherry Cola'. Anyway, it's a great song. As I'm writing this, I'm going down a rabbit hole of their best hits on YouTube. I'd recommend looking up 'Moon & Back' too – AWESOME SONG!

Anyhoo, I should also point out that this cupcake is the most drawn cupcake of all by you guys. I get tagged on Instagram at least twice a week from people who have drawn it. Every single drawing is different and amazing! BTW, if you guys draw my cupcakes, please feel free to tag me so I can see your amazing artwork. It makes me so happy!

10 white cupcake cases

CUPCAKES

- 1 batch Chocolate cupcakes (page 38)
- 175 ml (6 fl oz) cola
- 2 tablespoons cherry liqueur (optional)

CHOCOLATE SAUCE

- 250 ml (8½ fl oz/1 cup) Chocolate sauce (page 51)
- 2 tablespoons cherry brandy or 1 teaspoon cherry brandy flavouring

DECORATIONS

- 12 cherries (get the nice, shiny good-looking ones)

FROSTING

- 1 batch American buttercream frosting (page 45)
- 2 tablespoons cherry brandy or 1 teaspoon cherry brandy flavouring
- 2 drops pink food-gel colouring

CUPCAKES

When making the cupcake batter, replace the milk with cola and add the cherry liqueur, if using. Mix until well combined. Bake, then allow to cool.

CHOCOLATE SAUCE

Prepare the chocolate sauce by combining the sauce and brandy. Place in a squeeze bottle and set aside.

FROSTING

Make the frosting. Set about 3 tablespoons of plain frosting aside.

Add the cherry brandy or flavouring to the remaining frosting along with the pink food gel and mix until well combined.

ASSEMBLY

Core the centre of each cupcake with an apple corer (stop about 1 cm (½ in) from the bottom) and fill with chocolate sauce.

Fit the end of a piping bag with a Wilton 1M tip, fill with the pink frosting and pipe a swirl on top of each cupcake. Drizzle some chocolate sauce over the frosting and add a swirl of plain frosting (using a Wilton #32 tip) on top before you finish with a cherry.

MEDIUM

MAKES **10** CUPCAKES

10 white cupcake cases

STRAWBERRY GANACHE

400 g (14 oz) white chocolate chips
200 ml (7 fl oz) thickened (whipping) cream
2 drops pink food-gel colouring
1 teaspoon strawberry flavouring

MINI CHOCOLATE BARS

95 g (3¼ oz/½ cup) mini pink sprinkles
150 g (5½ oz) Wilton turquoise candy melts, melted

CUPCAKES & DOUGHNUTS

1 batch Vanilla cupcakes (page 34)
1 teaspoon strawberry flavouring
185 g (6½ oz/1 cup) rainbow confetti sprinkles

FROSTING

1 batch American buttercream frosting (page 45)

DECORATIONS

185 g (6½ oz/1 cup) assorted sprinkles of your choice
20 mini paper straws, to decorate (optional)

It's like Sunday in a cupcake!

STRAWBERRY GANACHE

Combine the white chocolate and cream in a microwave-safe bowl and microwave on high, for 20 seconds at a time, mixing well between each interval until smooth. Add the pink food gel and strawberry flavouring and mix until well combined. Cover with plastic wrap and set aside to cool at room temperature.

MINI CHOCOLATE BARS

Sprinkle some mini pink sprinkles into a mini chocolate bar silicone mould. Top with about 1 teaspoon of the melted turquoise candy and use a small offset spatula to spread it out. Chill for 10 minutes, then carefully remove from the mould once set.

CUPCAKES & DOUGHNUTS

Line a cupcake tin with the cupcake cases. Spray a doughnut tin with oil and use a paper towel to wipe away any excess. Set aside.

When making the cupcake batter, add the strawberry flavouring with the wet ingredients.

Once the batter is ready, fold in the confetti sprinkles.

Transfer the batter to a piping bag and snip off the end, ensuring that the hole is big enough to allow the confetti sprinkles through.

Pipe the batter into the doughnut baking tin, filling the moulds halfway. Give the tin a gentle tap to help any air bubbles at the bottom rise to the top.

Fill each cupcake case three-quarters of the way. Bake the doughnuts for 15 minutes and the cupcakes for 40 minutes. Allow the cupcakes to cool.

To get the doughnuts out of the hot doughnut tin, place a wire rack directly on top of the tin. Grip the tin and the rack with two tea towels (dish towels) and flip the tin over. Gently tap the base of the doughnut tin. This will allow the doughnuts to fall out easily without them ripping. It's best to do this as soon as they come out of the oven to stop them from cooking any further as the tin cools.

ASSEMBLY

Core the centre of each cupcake with an apple corer (stop about 1 cm (½ in) from the bottom) and fill with strawberry ganache.

Fit the end of a piping bag with a Wilton 6B tip, fill with the frosting and pipe a double-doughnut swirl (see page 14) on top. Drizzle over some strawberry ganache, then carefully push a doughnut into the frosting, in an upright position.

Drizzle more strawberry ganache over the doughnut and push a mini chocolate bar into the frosting in front of the doughnut. Finish with your choice of assorted sprinkles.

I also like to add little paper straws to the frosting to make it feel more like a freakshake.

Note
If it's a warm day, your frosting may not be firm enough to hold the doughnut. Try adding a paper straw behind your doughnut to stop it from tipping backwards, or secure the doughnut to the cake with a toothpick to help hold it in place. If you do use a toothpick, make sure your guests know there's a spear in the middle of their cupcake, otherwise there'll be trips to the emergency room!

See image on page 142.

FREAKFETTI *cupcakes*

BANANA HAMMOCK FREAKSHAKE *cake*

BANANA HAMMOCK FREAKSHAKE *cake*

MEDIUM

SERVES **30**

CHOCOLATE GANACHE

1 batch Chocolate ganache frosting (page 49)

CHOCOLATE CAKE

1 batch Chocolate cake (page 41)
4 ripe bananas, peeled and mashed
2 teaspoons banana flavouring
175 g (6 oz/1 cup) chocolate chips

BANANA CAKE

1 batch Vanilla cake (page 37)
1 teaspoon banana flavouring
10 drops yellow food-gel colouring
175 g (6 oz/1 cup) chocolate chips

BANANA DOUGHNUTS

1 batch Vanilla cupcakes (page 34)
3 teaspoons banana flavouring
10 drops yellow food-gel colouring
175 g (6 oz/1 cup) mini chocolate chips

CRUMB-COAT FROSTING

2 batches Swiss meringue buttercream frosting (page 46)
3 teaspoons banana flavouring

DECORATIONS

1 batch Chocolate sauce, to drizzle (page 51)
350 g (12½ oz/2 cups) mini chocolate chips
370 g (13 oz/2 cups) banana sprinkles
10 gold- and white-striped straws, cut in half to make smaller straws
10 yellow chocolate honeycomb candy balls

I'm so freaking excited to share this recipe with you guys! I've never made one of my freakshake cupcakes into a cake, and only people who have bought this book get to see the recipe. Yay!

CHOCOLATE GANACHE

When making the chocolate ganache, use milk chocolate instead of dark chocolate.

CHOCOLATE CAKE

Spray two 20 cm (8 in) cake tins with oil and line the bottoms with baking paper. Set aside.

When making the cake batter, add the mashed bananas and banana flavouring with the wet ingredients. Once the chocolate cake batter is ready, fold in the chocolate chips.

Divide the batter between the prepared tins and bake. Chill the cakes overnight.

BANANA CAKE

Spray two 20 cm (8 in) cake tins with oil and line the bottoms with baking paper. Set aside.

When making the cake batter, add the banana flavouring and yellow food gel with the wet ingredients.

Once the batter is ready, fold in the chocolate chips.

Divide the batter between the prepared tins and bake. Chill the cakes overnight.

BANANA DOUGHNUTS

Spray a doughnut tin with oil and use a paper towel to wipe away any excess. Set aside.

When making the batter, add the banana flavouring and yellow food gel with the wet ingredients.

Once the batter is ready, fold in the mini chocolate chips.

Transfer the batter to a piping bag and snip off the end, ensuring that the hole is big enough to allow the chocolate chips through.

Pipe the batter into the doughnut tin, filling the moulds halfway. Give the tin a gentle tap to help any air bubbles at the bottom rise to the top.

To get the doughnuts out of the hot doughnut tin, place a wire rack directly on top of the tin. Grip the tin and the rack with two tea towels (dish towels) and flip the tin over. Gently tap the base of the doughnut tin. This will allow the doughnuts to fall out easily without them ripping. It's best to do this as soon as they come out of the oven to stop them from cooking any further as the tin cools.

ASSEMBLY

Trim, fill and crumb-coat the cake (see page 10) using the crumb-coat frosting. When constructing the cake, alternate between chocolate and banana cake layers.

Use the chocolate ganache frosting for the outer layer of frosting (see page 12).

Add the banana sprinkles around the side of the cake – place more on the bottom and use fewer as you work your way up to create a sort of ombre effect.

Drizzle the top of the cake with the chocolate sauce.

Pile the banana cake doughnuts on top of the cake and drizzle each doughnut with the chocolate sauce. Add gold-striped straws in between some of the doughnuts. Finish off with yellow chocolate honeycomb candy balls.

See image on page 143.

REBEL PRIDE

'It's important to be visible.'

If you follow me on social media you'll know that music plays a really important role in my life. It inspires almost all of the cupcake designs you see on The Scran Line, and certainly all the ones in this chapter. Pop divas like Gaga, Beyoncé, Rihanna and Nicki Minaj are a constant source of inspiration for me. I love the way their music makes me feel empowered and confident. It's also taught me how to deal with life's ups and downs in a healthy way. I try to reflect that feeling in my desserts.

In 2002, I got my first taste of a pop diva with the arrival of a new artist named Christina Aguilera. The thing about Xtina is that she knows she has an amazing voice and she knows how to use it. Not only that, but every single song in her album *Stripped* was about embracing female sexuality and inner strength. That album instantly spoke to me. I still remember the feeling I had when I first heard the song 'Fighter'.

'Fighter' is an anthem for people who have experienced some really tough times. It's about the lessons you learn once you pull through and that, at the end of it all, you're left feeling like you can make it through anything. You're a fighter.

Continued ...

'Fighter' came out when I was still in high school and, even though that song and the entire album spoke to my soul, I was scared of openly listening to it. I was raised in a very conservative, religious household, and there were certain expectations about how to think and behave. In comes Xtina with her songs about sex, love, making mistakes, the lessons you learn from them and about living your truth.

Living your truth. I struggled with that for a very, very long time. It was a long, exhausting journey for me, but I eventually came out at age 25. And, even then, the process was very difficult, like it is for most people. The journey leading up to the day I came out was filled with constant fear and anxiety that people would find out I was gay. What would they say if they knew that I was gay? Would I lose my family? What would I do then? I already felt incredibly alone and so the thought of losing my family sent me into a deep depression.

I struggled with that depression on and off from ages 16 to 25. I became really good at hiding my unhappiness and who I was. Even from myself. As I got older though, that became a full-time job and it felt exhausting having to pretend to be someone else. At the age of 25, I finally reached out to an old high-school friend and that set me on a path to sorting out who I really was and how to navigate my way to happiness.

Let's go back to 2002. As infatuated as I was with Xtina's album, I was terrified that someone would hear me listening to it, so I made sure I listened to it at a low enough volume so nobody at home or at school would hear me. Boys didn't listen to Christina Aguilera. Only girls did. And the last thing I wanted was to be made fun of, or for people to know that I was different.

When I came out, that fear slowly went away because I didn't feel the need to hide what made me happy anymore. Now I'll listen to Gaga at full blast at the gym or while I'm shopping. Seriously. I go food shopping with my headphones in, and I'll have the volume up loud. Music makes me happy. People's opinions on what makes me happy matter very little to me.

If there are any young or old LGBTQI+ people reading this and they're on their journey of finding their happiness, my message to you is to worry less about others' opinions about what should make you happy. If you're a boy and putting on make-up makes you happy, then do it. Who said make-up was only for girls anyway? If you're a girl and you want to have short hair because that's what makes you happy, then do it. There's no rulebook on how girls or boys should speak, dress or act. If you're happy and healthy, then do what works best for you.

For me, that's shopping for butter while Gaga is screaming in my ears about how she kisses the bartender twice.

Like one of my favourite LGBTQI+ YouTubers says:

DANCING QUEEN *cupcakes*

MEDIUM

MAKES **15** CUPCAKES

INSPIRED BY: **DANCING QUEEN – ABBA**

15 white cupcake cases

CUPCAKES

1 batch Vanilla cupcakes (page 34)
2 teaspoons strawberry flavouring

COLOUR FORMULATIONS

red: 2 drops red food-gel colouring and 2 drops deep pink food-gel colouring
pink: 2 drops deep pink food-gel colouring
orange: 2 drops orange food-gel colouring and 1 drop yellow food-gel colouring
yellow: 3 drops yellow food-gel colouring
green: 2 drops teal food-gel colouring and 1 drop yellow food-gel colouring
blue: 1 drop sky blue food-gel colouring
purple: 2 drops deep purple food-gel colouring and 2 drops deep pink food-gel colouring

FROSTING

1 batch Swiss meringue buttercream frosting (page 46)
2 teaspoons strawberry flavouring

DECORATIONS

185 g (6½ oz/1 cup) assorted sprinkles of your choice
200 g (7 oz/⅓ cup) edible red glitter, for dusting

Everybody chill. I know there aren't seven colours in the rainbow, but you guys know I'm all about that OTT lyf, and I think pink should be in there! I mean, who doesn't?

CUPCAKES

When making the cupcake batter, add the strawberry flavouring with the wet ingredients.

Divide the batter between seven small bowls. Colour each one using the seven different colour formulations listed in the ingredients list.

Add the coloured batters to separate piping bags and pipe small blobs of each colour into the cupcake cases, filling them three-quarters of the way. Bake, then allow to cool.

FROSTING

Add the strawberry flavouring to the frosting and mix until well combined. Divide the frosting between seven small bowls and colour each one using the colour formulations listed in the ingredients list. Transfer the coloured frostings to separate piping bags.

Lay out a large sheet of plastic wrap on your workbench and pipe long lines of each coloured frosting in the order of the rainbow. Use the plastic wrap to help you roll up the frosting like a sushi roll into a log shape, then twist each end to secure. Snip off one end of the log and place it, cut side down, inside a piping bag fitted with a Wilton 8B tip.

ASSEMBLY

Core the centre of each cupcake with an apple corer (stop about 1 cm (½ in) from the bottom) and fill with your favourite sprinkles. Pipe a swirl of frosting on top of each cupcake and finish with a light dusting of edible glitter.

EASY

MAKES **20** CUPCAKES

INSPIRED BY: ***THE WIZARD OF OZ***

20 red foil cupcake cases

RED FROSTING

3 drops red food-gel colouring
3 drops pink food-gel colouring
¾ batch American buttercream frosting (page 45)

RAINBOW FROSTING

½ batch American buttercream frosting (page 45)
2 drops purple food-gel colouring
2 drops blue food-gel colouring
2 drops green food-gel colouring
2 drops yellow food-gel colouring
2 drops orange food-gel colouring
2 drops pink food-gel colouring

CUPCAKES

1 batch Vanilla cupcakes (page 34)
1 teaspoon strawberry flavouring
4 drops pink food-gel colouring
4 drops red food-gel colouring

DECORATIONS

200 g (7 oz/⅓ cup) edible red glitter

When I first heard the term 'Friend of Dorothy', I had no idea what it actually meant. I thought people were actually calling themselves friends of Dorothy – the character from *The Wizard Of Oz*. But no. It turns out that back in the '60s and '70s, even the '80s, when gay men were arrested for being gay, they developed their own language to stay safe. If you're trying to be stealthy but you want to know if someone is gay, you couldn't just ask, 'Are you gay?' What if that person was homophobic? Or a cop? Instead, you'd ask someone if they were a friend of Dorothy. The response 'Huh?' usually meant no. Yes meant, 'Yes I'm like you, it's safe to be around me'. I just love that so much. I mean, it sucks that people had to hide their true selves, but trust the gays to come up with their own language using pop-culture references!

RED FROSTING

Add the food gels to the frosting and mix until well combined.

RAINBOW FROSTING

To make the rainbow frosting, divide it between six smaller bowls and colour each one using the colours listed in the ingredients list. Transfer to separate piping bags and snip off the ends.

CUPCAKES

When making the cupcake batter, add the strawberry flavouring and food gels with the wet ingredients. Bake, then allow to cool.

ASSEMBLY

Core the centre of each cupcake with an apple corer (stop about 1 cm (½ in) from the bottom) and fill with purple frosting, then blue and, finally, green. Pipe little blobs of yellow, orange and pink frosting first on top of the cupcake, then on top of each other. Chill for 20 minutes.

Fit the end of a piping bag with a Wilton 6B star tip, fill with the red frosting and pipe a tall swirl around the rainbow. Chill for 20 minutes.

Use a teaspoon to carefully sprinkle red glitter all over the frosting.

FEMME QUEEN REALNESS - THE REALNESS *cupcakes*

MEDIUM

MAKES **20** CUPCAKES

INSPIRED BY: **CATEGORY IS – RUPAUL**

20 white cupcake cases

CUPCAKES

1 batch Vanilla cupcakes (page 34)
1 teaspoon strawberry flavouring
3 drops pink food-gel colouring

PINK PRINCESS CROWNS

300 g (10½ oz) Wilton pink candy melts
1 teaspoon edible pink glitter or pink lustre dust

FROSTING

3 drops pink food-gel colouring
1 teaspoon strawberry flavouring
¾ batch American buttercream frosting (page 45)
100 edible diamantes (can be purchased online)

When I was younger and I was just starting to realise that I was gay, I was afraid of anyone finding out. That fear stemmed from my conservative upbringing, where being gay was wrong and where effeminate guys were weirdos. Of course, none of that is true. As I eventually began to learn more about who I was and to embrace it, I began to let go of my fear of the LGBTQI+ community. I got to meet many different types of people, and the one thing they all had in common was that they were all living their truth. These cupcakes are a celebration of people living their true, authentic selves.

Oh, by the way, my sister and I used to play kings and queens when we were little and she always had the longest piece of material because she was the queen. I was always secretly jealous. Guess who grew up to be a Kween?

CUPCAKES

When making the cupcake batter, add the strawberry flavouring and pink food gel with the wet ingredients. Bake, then allow to cool.

PINK PRINCESS CROWNS

Start by melting the pink candy.

Place a large sheet of baking paper on your workbench. Pour over the melted candy and use a large spatula to spread it out evenly. Let it set before brushing with some edible pink glitter.

Use a large, sharp knife dipped in some hot water to cut the chocolate into diamond shapes about the size of your pinkie finger. Cut a few smaller ones as well.

FROSTING

Add the pink food gel and strawberry flavouring to the frosting and mix until well combined.

ASSEMBLY

Fit the end of a piping bag with a large round tip, fill with half the frosting and pipe low bulbs of frosting on top of each cupcake.

Fit the end of another piping bag with a Wilton 1M tip, fill with the remaining frosting and frost smaller bulbs of frosting on top of the low bulbs until covered. Stick enough pink candy shards in each cupcake to form a crown shape.

Carefully add two rings of diamantes around the frosting.

MEDIUM

MAKES **20**

INSPIRED BY: **KITTY GIRL – RUPAUL**

20 white cupcake cases

CAT EYES

100 g (3½ oz) Wilton black candy melts, melted
20 g (¾ oz) Wilton pink candy melts, melted

CUPCAKES

1 batch Vanilla cupcakes (page 34)
1 teaspoon melon flavouring
2 drops pink food-gel colouring
2 drops turquoise food-gel colouring

PINK FROSTING

2 teaspoons strawberry flavouring
3 drops pink food-gel colouring
½ batch American buttercream frosting (page 45)

COLOURED FROSTING

1 teaspoon melon flavouring
1 batch American buttercream frosting (page 45)
2 drops green food-gel colouring
2 drops deep pink food-gel colouring
2 drops pink food-gel colouring
2 drops purple food-gel colouring

DECORATIONS

20 pink mini marshmallows, halved

Hey kitty girl! At the end of every season of *RuPaul's Drag Race,* the three or four final queens do a music video together of one of Ru's songs and this is, by far, my fave one! YouTube it. It's got Trixie Mattel who I love, love, love! In fact, if you watch it, you'll notice that Nicki Star Tip (page 167) and her have something in common!

CAT EYES

Draw some cat eyes on a piece of paper. Place the paper underneath a large piece of baking paper.

Transfer the melted candy to separate piping bags fitted with Wilton #4 piping tips.

Begin by piping two little blobs of pink food gel next to each other over the pupils. They'll be the little sparkle in your cat eyes.

Pipe the cat eye shapes in black over the pink blobs and allow them to set at room temperature. Repeat until you have forty cat eyes.

CUPCAKES

When making the cupcake batter, add the melon flavouring with the wet ingredients.

Divide the batter between two mixing bowls. Add the pink food gel to one bowl and colour the second bowl with the turquoise food gel. Mix well. Transfer the coloured batters to two piping bags and snip off the ends. Pipe thin squiggles of each colour into the cupcake cases, alternating the colours, until the cupcake cases are filled three-quarters of the way. Bake, then allow to cool.

PINK FROSTING

Add the strawberry flavouring and pink food gel to the frosting and mix until well combined. Transfer to a piping bag fitted with a large round tip.

COLOURED FROSTING

To prepare the frosting, add the melon flavouring to the frosting and mix until well combined.

Divide the frosting between four mixing bowls and colour each one using the colours listed in the ingredients list.

Transfer the coloured frostings to separate piping bags fitted with Wilton #4 tips.

ASSEMBLY

To finish the cupcakes, frost a tall bulb of pink frosting on top of each cupcake using a large round tip, then pipe long hairs of each coloured frosting on the bulb. Add two cat-eyes to the front of each bulb. Finish with two marshmallow halves to make the cat ears.

CELEBRATE GOOD TIMES *cake*

HARD

SERVES **30**

INSPIRED BY: **CELEBRATION – KYLIE MINOGUE**

WHITE CHOCOLATE SPHERES

100 g (3½ oz) Wilton turquoise candy melts and 1 tablespoon coconut or vegetable oil, melted
100 g (3½ oz) Wilton pink candy melts and 1 tablespoon coconut or vegetable oil, melted
100 g (3½ oz) Wilton orange candy melts and 1 tablespoon coconut or vegetable oil, melted
400 g (14 oz) white cooking chocolate and 1 tablespoon coconut or vegetable oil, melted
1 tablespoon melted white chocolate

CAKE

2 batches Vanilla cake (page 37)
2 teaspoons raspberry flavouring
orange: 2 drops orange food-gel colouring and 1 drop yellow food-gel colouring
yellow: 3 drops yellow food-gel colouring
green: 2 drops teal food-gel colouring and 1 drop yellow food-gel colouring
blue: 1 drop sky blue food-gel colouring
purple: 2 drops deep purple food-gel colouring and 2 drops deep pink food-gel colouring
pink: 2 drops deep pink food-gel colouring
red: 2 drops red food-gel colouring and 2 drops deep pink food-gel colouring

Ceeeeelebrate good times! Yahoo! I love, love, love this song! Kylie is such a huge gay icon and such an iconic Australian artist. This song just makes me feel happy and super gay! This cake would be perfect for any pride celebration.

WHITE CHOCOLATE SPHERES

For this recipe, you'll be making one large chocolate sphere (two half spheres) and two small chocolate spheres (four half spheres). To make the spheres, you'll need the following moulds:

Large sphere mould: polycarbonate chocolate mould half-sphere 10 cm (4 in), 2 cavities.

Small sphere mould: polycarbonate chocolate mould half-sphere 5 cm (2 in), 8 cavities.

Place the different coloured candy melts and coconut oil into separate microwave-safe bowls and microwave on high, for 20 seconds at a time, mixing well between each interval until smooth.

Splatter the turquoise, pink and orange candy inside the moulds, then refrigerate for 15 minutes, or until completely set. Pour the white chocolate into the moulds, filling them up about halfway. Use the back of a teaspoon to spread the chocolate up the sides. Turn the moulds upside-down over a baking tray and allow any excess chocolate to drip out. Chill for 40 minutes.

The chocolate spheres should come out easily. To put them together, briefly place the rim of one half in a warm frying pan to soften and melt the chocolate ever so slightly. Press the other half of the mould to the melted sphere and stick them together. Wipe away any excess chocolate around the seam with your finger. Hold the halves together to allow them to set a little before popping them in the fridge to set completely. Repeat the process to make the smaller spheres.

CAKE

For this recipe, you'll be making seven rainbow-coloured 20 cm (8 in) cakes. As a baker who bakes every day, I have eight 20 cm (8 in) cake tins but, if you only have one, you can still make this cake, it'll just take a little while.

To make the cake, add the raspberry flavouring with the wet ingredients.

FROSTING

3 batches Swiss meringue buttercream frosting (page 46)
3 teaspoons raspberry flavouring

Once the batter is ready, divide it between seven smaller bowls. You can do this using a pair of kitchen scales to weigh out the batter, or by using an ice-cream scoop to evenly distribute the batter, which I find easier. Colour each bowl of batter a separate colour following the colour formulations in the ingredients list.

Fill each 20 cm (8 in) cake tin with one of the rainbow colours. Bake, then allow to cool.

FROSTING

Prepare the frosting by adding the raspberry flavouring to the frosting and mix until well combined.

Trim, fill and crumb-coat the cake (see page 10) using 1½ batches of frosting and making sure the cake layers are arranged in the order of the rainbow. Chill for 1 hour.

Use the rest of the frosting to add the final layer to the cake (see page 12).

TO DECORATE

To finish off the cake, splatter the frosting with the melted turquoise, pink and orange candy. Dab a small amount of white chocolate on the top of the cake to help stick on the white chocolate spheres.

See image on page 160.

CELEBRATE GOOD TIMES *cake*

I remember when I was at kindergarten. One of my favourite things to do was paint. Oh, by the way, I was always able to colour inside the lines at kindy – #humblebrag. The best thing I ever painted was this rainbow splatter thing. We had these big sheets of paper and we got to splatter paint on them with a big brush. The teacher put our names on them and let them dry. The next day, they were all folded up and put into big envelopes where we stored our work from the year. I still vividly remember that. That's what inspired these macarons. Fast forward to today, and those rainbow dots mean something different to me.

MEDIUM

MAKES **30** SANDWICHED MACARONS

MACARONS

1 batch Vanilla macarons (page 42)

FROSTING

2 teaspoons strawberry flavouring
1 batch American buttercream frosting (page 45)
red: 2 drops red food-gel colouring and 2 drops deep pink food-gel colouring
orange: 2 drops orange food-gel colouring and 1 drop yellow food-gel colouring
yellow: 3 drops yellow food-gel colouring
green: 2 drops teal food-gel colouring and 1 drop yellow food-gel colouring
blue: 1 drop sky blue food-gel colouring
purple: 2 drops deep purple food-gel colouring and 2 drops deep pink food-gel colouring

DECORATIONS

liquid food dye, for splattering (pink, blue and yellow)

MACARONS

Prepare the vanilla macarons.

FROSTING

Add the strawberry flavouring to the frosting and mix until well combined. Divide the frosting between six small bowls and colour each one using the colour formulations listed in the ingredients list. Transfer the coloured frostings to separate piping bags.

Lay out a large sheet of plastic wrap onto your workbench and pipe long lines of each coloured frosting in the listed order. Use the plastic wrap to help you roll the frosting up like a sushi roll into a log shape, then twist each end to secure. Snip off one end of the log and place it, cut side down, inside a piping bag fitted with a Wilton #32 tip. Set aside.

ASSEMBLY

To finish the macarons, lay out the macaron shells on a piece of baking paper and splatter with different-coloured food dye. You might want to mix the food dye with some vodka or vanilla extract to help thin it out a little. Leave to dry.

Pipe a swirl of rainbow frosting on the flat side of half the macaron shells and sandwich with the remaining shells.

See image on page 161.

HEY NICK,

I get loads of emails and questions in the comments section of my posts, and I do my best to answer as many of them as I can. Here's a list of the most common questions you guys ask and some funny ones that I wanted to include for a laugh.

You can always ask me questions through my website, www.thescranline.com, or on social media :)

BAKING QUESTIONS

What advice would you give to an aspiring pastry chef/baker?

Always have fun. Don't do it for any other reason other than loving it, otherwise it will drain the life out of you as it's a lot of work. Also make sure you measure everything out super accurately and have everything measured before you start a recipe.

Which of your recipes is the best for beginners/ doesn't have complex ingredients?

Good question! Try my plain chocolate or red velvet cupcakes if you're a beginner. You can find those recipes in the Rebels Basics chapter (page 31).

What are your baking essentials? Every time I buy a must-have item, I need another one, so what would be your list to help noob bakers like me?

OK, I get asked this one a lot. Here are my top three baking tools:

1. **Spatula.** Make sure it's a good one, not a cheap plastic one. Invest in at least three good-quality spatulas for your kitchen. Most commercial kitchen-supply stores will sell the really good ones. Look for something with a strong handle and a rubber end that's not too soft.
2. **Scissors.** Seems like a simple one, right? I cannot tell you how many scissors I've used that don't actually cut! How does anyone get away with making scissors that don't cut?! Get a good pair of scissors and keep them in the same place, because we all know they're easy to lose.
3. **Ice-cream scoop.** If you're into baking, then having an ice-cream scoop is important. Besides scooping out ridiculous amounts of ice cream when you're going through a break up, they do loads of other things. One of the most common things I use them for is to fill my cupcake cases with batter. When you use an ice-cream scoop, it ensures everything is filled up with the same amount of batter so that everything takes the same time to bake. I also use an ice-cream scoop to split my batter up if I'm colouring it different colours. Sure, you can weigh it, but scooping it is so much easier, and quicker too.

What oven do you use? What's the brand?

The oven my apartment came with. It's not a big-brand oven, so sharing the brand would be pointless because unless you're in Melbourne, you're not likely to be able to get it. But the important thing to keep in mind if you're buying a new oven is that you want an electric fan-forced oven. Gas ovens are not as good for baking cakes.

What food colourings do you use?

I use either Americolor food gels or Chef Master.

Does activated charcoal alter the flavour of the recipes much?

Actually, it doesn't have any flavour at all!

Can your cupcake recipes be turned into mini cupcakes?

Yes! They can. Bake them for half the amount of time.

How do you get your cupcakes to have a round dome? Mine always crack and look like a volcano.

It's all about temperature control. If your cupcakes are cracking, browning or rising like mountains, it's because your oven temperature is too high. I like to bake on a low, slow heat, which gives my cupcakes time to rise slowly, and they don't brown and crack. If you're finding that even with the right temperature your oven is still doing those things, lower it again by about 10°C (50°F). Every oven is different.

On average, how long does it take to bake one of your cakes?

It takes me two days. It can be done in one day, but I like to make baking as stress-free as possible, so I prefer to bake the cake the night before I decorate it. I like to work with cakes that are completely chilled.

What is the best way to make a cake in advance?

Prep as much as you can in advance. Bake the cakes the day before. That way, all you need to do on the day is decorate your cake.

REBEL KWEENS

Attention: this is Nick speaking. Nicki doesn't know I'm putting this in here. Don't tell her. I often get a lot of hate online for some of the sassy replies I give to people who confuse constructive criticism with back-handed compliments. Nick, you talk too much. Nick, you're fat. You're too gay, why are your eyes weird? I like to have fun when I reply to those people. Some people confuse my sassy replies with rudeness. Oh henny, you think that's sassy? Meet the Sassatron herself.

NICKI STAR TIP

THE KWEEN IS COMING FOR HUH CROWN.

Hey guys, I'm beautiful, thank you.

Nick asked me to write a short thing in his stupid book. 'Cos like, I'm super famous and he's got no talent, so this will obvs help him sell books.

I just wanna say first of all, if you see me in the street, please don't say hello 'cos like, I'm not even bragging, but I'm too famous for you. But, if you do see me in public, take photos (obvs from a 300-metre distance), but send them to me online so I can see if I look good first. If you don't hear from my lawyer, then you can post them.

OMG guys, you don't even know, I had to fight so hard to even get a makeover for this book. Like, as if I was gonna be in the book without getting a Thai face slap or a bee-venom mask. It's not unreasonable to expect an Amazonian fish pedicure is it?

I got them in the end, that's why I look so beautiful in these photos.

Anyway, the only reason I agreed to do Nick's stupid cookbook is because he's paying me millions of dollars. I don't need the money, but like I don't not need it either 'cos looking this good isn't cheap. And I need to look beautiful 'cos I've met the man of my dreams and he's a billionaire. At least he says he is. I love him and everything, but if he didn't have billions of dollars I don't know what would happen to that love.

I'm writing this on my first-class flight back to LA 'cos he said we needed to talk. He sounded really sad on the phone, but I think it's because he's so sad about how much money he's spent on an engagement ring. OMG guys, I think I'm gonna get engaged. If he thinks I'm taking his name though, he's got another thing coming.

Kisses x

GET INTO THE GROOVE *cupcakes*

MEDIUM

MAKES **15** CUPCAKES

INSPIRED BY: **GET INTO THE GROOVE – MADONNA**

15 white cupcake cases

CUPCAKES

1 batch Vanilla cupcakes (page 34)
1 teaspoon lime flavouring
3 drops green food-gel colouring
1 tablespoon unsweetened (Dutch) cocoa powder and 4 drops black food-gel colouring

FROSTING

3 drops pink food-gel colouring
1 teaspoon strawberry flavouring
1 batch American buttercream frosting (page 45)

GROOVY DECORATIONS

250 g (9 oz/2 cups) icing (confectioners') sugar
2½ tablespoons powdered egg whites
3 drops blue food-gel colouring
4 drops yellow food-gel colouring
6 drops black food-gel colouring
2 drops pink food-gel colouring

Did you know that 'voguing' was discovered by Madonna on a trip to a gay club? The gays were doing it and then she turned it into a dance move and it went mainstream. Madonna became an instant gay icon with that song and basically all of her other songs. That's why she's a Kween! My fave Madonna songs are from her '80s era. 'Get Into The Groove' is one of the best ones from that era. These cupcakes are perfect for Madonna fans or even for your next '80s-themed party!

CUPCAKES

When making the cupcake batter, add the lime flavouring with the wet ingredients.

Divide the batter between two bowls. Colour one with the green food gel and the second with the cocoa powder and black food gel and mix until well combined. Transfer the batters to separate piping bags.

Pipe random layers of green and black batter into the cupcake cases, filling them three-quarters of the way. Pipe the colours on top of each other and don't be too neat; you want to get that zebra effect. Bake, then allow to cool.

FROSTING

Add the pink food gel and strawberry flavouring to the frosting and mix until well combined.

GROOVY DECORATIONS

Line two baking trays with baking paper and set aside.

You can make the royal icing using a stand mixer fitted with the paddle attachment, or you can use a hand mixer.

Add the icing sugar and powdered egg whites to a large mixing bowl and mix on low speed until combined. Add 1 tablespoon of water and mix. You want the mixture to be thin enough to pipe, but stiff enough to hold its shape and not be a runny mess. If it is too stiff, add 1 teaspoon of water at a time until you reach the right consistency.

Transfer one-third of the mixture to a small bowl and add the blue food gel. Mix until well combined. Colour the second third with yellow food gel and mix. Split the remaining icing in half. Colour one half black and the other half pink. Transfer the coloured icings to separate piping bags fitted with Wilton #4 tips.

Begin by piping different-sized blue circles (no bigger than 2 cm/¾ in) on the baking paper. Pipe little pink dots inside them and leave to set at room temperature.

To make the yellow triangles, pipe yellow triangles on the baking paper, then pipe little dots of black icing inside them. Allow them to set completely before piping a black triangle shadow on two sides of each triangle.

You'll need about ten circles and ten triangles per cupcake. Guys, these can take a while, so throw on your fave Madonna album or a podcast and pipe for your life!

ASSEMBLY

To assemble, fit the end of a piping bag with a Wilton 1M tip, fill with the pink frosting and pipe a swirl of frosting on top of each cupcake. To finish, stick the circle and triangle shapes into the frosting.

See image on page 170.

GET INTO THE GROOVE *cupcakes*

DIAMOND HEART *cupcakes*

DIAMOND HEART *cupcakes*

HARD

MAKES **20** CUPCAKES

INSPIRED BY: **DIAMOND HEART – LADY GAGA**

20 white cupcake cases

CUPCAKE ELEMENTS

Cupcakes (can be made the day before)
Turkish delight centre (can be made the day before)
Frosting in mould (can be made the day before)
Mirror glaze (must be made on the day and used to cover the frosting)
Candy shards (can be made the day before)

CUPCAKES

1 batch Vanilla cupcakes (page 34)
2 teaspoons coconut flavouring

TURKISH DELIGHT GEL

35 g (1¼ oz) cornflour (cornstarch)
200 g (7 oz) granulated sugar
1 drop pink food-gel colouring
1 teaspoon rose flavouring

CANDY SHARDS

350 g (12½ oz/2 cups) Wilton pink candy melts

OK, so here's the story on these cupcakes: I create content for a company based in LA named Tastemade. They were approached by Gaga's people a couple of weeks before her Super Bowl performance in 2017. Tastemade emailed me and asked me to create a cupcake to help celebrate Gaga being at the game and that it was going to be delivered to Gaga herself. I was so excited, I just about left a Nick-shaped hole in the wall. I started jumping and crying as if I'd just won the *Price Is Right*.

So, I created this cupcake, which tied in with her new album, *Joanne*. The colours were inspired by the hat she wore on the album cover and the name was inspired by the album's opening track. The sharp shards are inspired by the '80s punk-rock fashion of her previous albums.

Tastemade made the cupcakes for her, delivered them to her and put a little note inside from me. Here's a screenshot of her tweet back to me.

It's one of the proudest moments of my life. I got to create a cupcake for Lady Gaga – someone who I have looked up to, felt inspired by, and whose music makes me feel empowered as a gay man.

CUPCAKES

When making the cupcake batter, add the coconut flavouring with the wet ingredients. Bake, then allow to cool.

TURKISH DELIGHT GEL

Combine the cornflour with 80 ml (2½ fl oz/⅓ cup) water and mix well. Set aside.

Add the sugar and 375 ml (12½ fl oz/1½ cups) water to a saucepan and bring to the boil. Reduce the heat to medium and add the cornflour mixture. Mix for 5 minutes until it thickens. Add the pink food gel and rose flavouring and mix until evenly coloured.

Transfer the mixture to a bowl and chill until set. Once set, pass the mixture through a fine-mesh sieve to return it to a gel consistency.

MIRROR GLAZE

20 g (¾ oz) powdered gelatin
200 ml (7 fl oz) sweetened condensed milk
300 g (10½ oz) granulated sugar
350 g (12½ oz/2 cups) white chocolate chips
½ drop mauve food-gel colouring
1 drop pink food-gel colouring
10 drops bright white food-gel colouring
1 teaspoon coconut flavouring

FROSTING

2 teaspoons rose flavouring
1 batch American buttercream frosting (page 45)

See image on page 171.

CANDY SHARDS

Place the pink candy melts in a microwave-safe bowl and microwave on high, for 20 seconds at a time, mixing well in-between each interval until smooth.

Pour the melted candies onto a baking tray lined with baking paper and spread them out as thinly as possible using a large offset spatula. Take care not to wrinkle the baking paper. Allow to set at room temperature.

Run a large knife under hot water, then dry with a tea towel (dish towel). Cut out shards, making sure each shard looks thin in appearance and has four sides.

MIRROR GLAZE

Combine the gelatin and 125 ml (4 fl oz/½ cup) water in a small mixing bowl and set aside for 5 minutes.

Heat the milk, sugar and 150 ml (5 fl oz) water in a saucepan over a medium heat and bring to a simmer. Add the gelatin and stir until dissolved.

Place the chocolate chips in a large, heatproof bowl. Pour the hot milk mixture over the chocolate and let it sit for 5 minutes. Once the chocolate has softened, use a hand-held blender to smooth out the mixture. Add the food gels and coconut flavouring and mix until well combined. Pass the mixture through a fine-mesh sieve to remove any remaining lumps. Leave the glaze to cool to 33°C (91°F) before using.

FROSTING

Add the rose flavouring to the frosting and mix until well combined. Transfer to a piping bag and snip off the end.

Pipe about 3 tablespoons of frosting into a six-cavity half-sphere silicone mould (see page 22). Use the back of a teaspoon to spread the frosting out nice and evenly. Fill the centres with frosting and use a large offset spatula to spread it out evenly. Freeze for 1 hour.

Carefully invert the moulds to release the frosting spheres. Repeat until you have made twenty half-spheres.

Turn a glass upside down on a baking tray and put a frosting sphere on top. Pour the mirror glaze over the top of the sphere, allowing any excess to run down the glass. Repeat with the remaining frosting spheres, then carefully transfer then to a baking tray lined with baking paper and refrigerate for 1 hour to set.

ASSEMBLY

Core the centre of each cupcake with an apple corer (stop about 1 cm (½ in) from the bottom) and fill with Turkish delight gel.

Pipe a small bulb of leftover frosting on top of each cupcake. This will help the frosting spheres stick. Use a small offset spatula to transfer the mirror-glazed spheres to the tops of the cupcakes.

Finish off by sticking pink candy shards to the mirror glaze, leaving some of the mirror glaze exposed.

GALAXY SPACE TIME *cupcakes*

EASY

MAKES **10** CUPCAKES

INSPIRED BY: **VENUS – LADY GAGA**

10 silver-foil cupcake cases

CUPCAKES

1 batch Chocolate cupcakes (page 38)

FROSTING

5 drops black food-gel colouring
1 batch chocolate-flavoured Swiss meringue buttercream frosting (page 46)

DECORATIONS

2 tablespoons silver lustre dust
80 ml (2½ fl oz/⅓ cup) vodka or vanilla extract
50 g (1¾ oz) silver-star sprinkles

We're talking '60s silver space-suit realness with this cupcake.

CUPCAKES

Prepare the chocolate cupcakes. Bake, then allow to cool

FROSTING

Add the black food gel to the chocolate buttercream and mix until well combined. It should come out a dark grey.

ASSEMBLY

Fit the end of a piping bag with a Wilton 8B tip, fill with the frosting and pipe a soft-serve swirl (page 14) on top of your cupcakes. Chill for an hour or so to allow the frosting to stiffen up.

Combine the silver lustre dust and vodka in a small mixing bowl and mix until well combined. Use a small, food-safe paintbrush to brush the chilled frosting with random strokes of silver paint. Finish with a sprinkle of silver-star sprinkles.

PLATINUM BLONDE *cupcakes*

EASY

MAKES **20** CUPCAKES

20 white cupcake cases

CUPCAKES

1 batch Vanilla cupcakes (page 34)
1 teaspoon musk flavouring
1 drop purple food-gel colouring
1 drop pink food-gel colouring

FROSTING

1 teaspoon musk flavouring
1 drop purple food-gel colouring
1 drop pink food-gel colouring
1 batch Swiss meringue buttercream frosting (page 46)

DECORATION

300 g (10½ oz) white Persian fairy floss/ cotton candy (Pashmak)

Your make up is terrible, but I love you anywayyyyy! That sums up Alaska. I love, love, love Alaska! She's one of my fave drag queens. When I first heard her talk on *RuPaul's Drag Race* I was kind of annoyed. She talks so slow and really LA Valleygirl. What I love about her is that she's super smart, really funny and she's an amazing artist. In fact, she has a song called 'This Is My Hair'. In it, she basically repeats the same words over and over again, but there are some really funny lyrics in there too. One of my faves is: 'I am naturally a platinum blonde', which, of course, she isn't. But she's a drag queen, so she can be whatever she likes. These cupcakes are in honour of Alaska and her platinum blonde hair.

CUPCAKES

When making the cupcake batter, add the musk flavouring and food gels with the wet ingredients. Bake, then allow to cool.

FROSTING

Add the musk flavouring and food gels to the frosting and mix until well combined.

ASSEMBLY

Fit the end of a piping bag with a medium round tip, fill it with the frosting and pipe a thin swirl or tall bulb of frosting on top of each cupcake. This is going to act as a support for the fairy floss. Carefully wrap the fairy floss around the frosting. This can be done 1–2 hours before serving. Persian fairy floss lasts a lot longer than regular fairy floss, but it will still melt when exposed to any moisture.

HARD

MAKES **10** CUPCAKES

INSPIRED BY: **IF I COULD TURN BACK TIME – CHER**

10 brown cupcake cases

CANDY SHARDS

300 g (10½ oz) Wilton black candy melts
½ teaspoon edible black shimmer powder

FROSTING

1 batch chocolate-flavoured American buttercream frosting (page 45)
1 tablespoon food-safe activated charcoal

CUPCAKES

1 batch Chocolate cupcakes (page 38)
1 tablespoon food-safe activated charcoal

Fun story: my fave song when I was little was 'If I Could Turn Back Time' by Cher. The OG pop diva. And I still love that song. If you haven't seen the music video, I'd recommend taking a look, I mean, it's tragic in a good way. This cupcake is inspired by the outfit she wore in that music video and the lighting used in it too!

CANDY SHARDS

Put the candy melts in a microwave-safe bowl and microwave on high, for 20 seconds at a time, mixing well between each interval until melted.

Pour the melted candy onto a tray lined with a sheet of baking paper and use a large offset spatula to spread it out evenly. Leave to set at room temperature.

Once set, brush with edible black shimmer powder using a food-safe paintbrush. Dip a large knife in warm water and dry it off, then cut the candy into small diamonds about the size of a fingernail.

Refrigerate for 1 hour to chill before separating the diamond shards.

FROSTING

Combine the frosting and charcoal in a large mixing bowl. Mix until really well combined, making sure you scrape down the side of the bowl at least once.

CUPCAKES

When making the cupcake batter, add the charcoal with the dry ingredients. Bake, then allow to cool.

ASSEMBLY

Fit the end of a piping bag with a Wilton 8B tip, fill with black chocolate frosting and pipe a soft-serve swirl of frosting (page 14) on top of each cupcake. Arrange the chocolate diamonds in a V-shape on top of the frosting.

HARD

SERVES **30**

INSPIRED BY: **#LEMONADE – BEYONCÉ**

JELLY JEWELS

400 ml (13½ fl oz) cold water
100 g (3½ oz) powdered gelatin
500 ml (17 fl oz/2 cups) lemon juice, fresh or ready squeezed
125 g (4½ oz) granulated sugar

FROSTING

20 drops yellow food-gel colouring
3 tablespoons shop-bought lemon curd or 3 teaspoons lemon flavouring
4 batches Swiss meringue buttercream frosting (page 46)

CAKE

2 batches Vanilla cake (page 37)
zest of 2 lemons
125 ml (4 fl oz/½ cup) lemon juice
10 drops yellow food-gel colouring

When life gives you lemons, make a #lemonade cake. Well, that's not how it actually goes, but you get the drift. And yes, this is a Beyoncé-inspired cake. Beyoncé's *Lemonade* album dropped one day (something she's now known for doing), and I was instantly obsessed. There are so many amazing messages in that album, I'd recommend giving it a listen.

JELLY JEWELS

Combine the water and gelatin in a large mixing bowl and mix until well combined. Leave it to sit for 2 minutes.

Add the lemon juice and sugar to a microwave-safe bowl and microwave on high for 3 minutes. Add the gelatin mixture to the lemon juice and stir until completely dissolved. Spray a jewel mould (see page 22) with oil and wipe away any excess with a paper towel. Fill the moulds with the jelly mixture and chill for 3 hours.

An easier way of making the jellies that doesn't require a mould is to simply use a 20 × 20 cm (8 × 8 in) cake tin. Lightly spray the tin with oil and gently wipe it down before adding the lemon jelly mixture. Once the jelly has set, turn the jelly slab out onto a chopping board and use a large knife to cut the jellies into ice cube-sized dice. Set aside.

FROSTING

Add the yellow food gel and lemon curd to the frosting and mix until well combined.

CAKE

When making the cake batter, add the lemon zest, lemon juice and yellow food gel with the wet ingredients. Bake, then allow to cool.

Trim, fill and crumb-coat the cake (see page 10), then chill for 2 hours. Add the final layer of frosting (see page 12), reserving some frosting for the final decorations. Chill for another 2 hours.

TO DECORATE

To add the final decorations to the cake, fit the end of a piping bag with a Wilton #4 round tip, fill it with the remaining frosting and draw large geometric shapes on the outside of the cake. Fill the shapes in with more lines. This can take a while. Put on a Beyoncé album and pipe for YO LIFE! And Don't F it up! #RuPaul

To finish the cake, top with a pile of the jellies up to 1 hour before serving.

CATCHING FEELINGS *macarons*

EASY

MAKES **15** SANDWICHED MACARONS

INSPIRED BY: **ALL EYES ON YOU – MEEK MILLS FT. NICKI MINAJ**

MACARONS

1 batch Vanilla macarons (page 42)
3 tablespoons food-safe activated charcoal

FROSTING

3 tablespoons food-safe activated charcoal
1 batch chocolate-flavoured Swiss meringue buttercream frosting (page 46)

DECORATION

90 blackberries (you'll need about six blackberries for each macaron – they're big macarons)

This is all about macaron sexiness: black and shiny, making those juicy berries pop with gloss.

MACARONS

Add the charcoal powder with the icing sugar and almond flour and pulse in a food processor until well combined.

When piping the macarons, pipe them 5 cm (2 in) in diameter. Allow to dry, then bake. Allow to cool.

FROSTING

To prepare the frosting, add the charcoal to the chocolate buttercream and mix until well combined.

ASSEMBLY

Fit the end of a piping bag with a large round tip, fill with the frosting and pipe a bulb of frosting, about as tall as your blackberries, in the centre of the flat side of half the macaron shells. Arrange blackberries around the edge of the macaron shells, then sandwich with the remaining shells.

EASY

MAKES **30** SANDWICHED MACARONS

INSPIRED BY: **PINK PRINT – NICKI MINAJ**

MACARONS

1 batch Vanilla macarons (page 42)
8 drops deep pink food-gel colouring

DECORATIONS

2 sheets edible gold leaf
200 g (7 oz) raspberry jam
200 g (7 oz) freeze-dried raspberries, crushed

FROSTING

1 batch Chocolate ganache frosting (page 49)

These ones are inspired by my favourite Nicki Minaj album, *Pink Print*. You know how when you listen to a song it reminds you of a time in your life or a specific moment? This album came out around the time I first went to New York. It was freezing cold and I was walking up the Brooklyn Bridge as I was listening to it. Every time I hear this album I get a flash of the Brooklyn Bridge. It's weird, but I love it!

MACARONS

When making the meringue, add the pink food gel at about the 3-minute mark. Bake, then allow to cool.

To apply the gold leaf to your baked macaron shells, dab your finger in a tiny bit of water and very gently sweep it across the top of each shell. Stick the gold leaf on top.

ASSEMBLY

Fit the end of a piping bag with a Wilton 6B tip, fill with the ganache and pipe a ring of ganache on the flat side of half the macaron shells. Fill the holes with some raspberry jam and sandwich with the remaining shells. Gently roll the exposed frosting in some crushed freeze-dried raspberries.

DIVAS GETTING MONEY *macarons*

EASY

MAKES **30** SANDWICHED MACARONS

MACARONS

1 batch Vanilla macarons (page 42)
2 drops gold food-gel colouring
2 drops yellow food-gel colouring
2 drops orange food-gel colouring
2 drops purple food-gel colouring

GOLD PAINT

5 teaspoons gold lustre dust
200 ml (7 fl oz) vodka or vanilla extract

FROSTING

1 batch Chocolate ganache frosting (page 49)

Tell me something … where yo boss at? OK, so let me explain how much Beyoncé means to me and why. Let's start with a PSA she was a part of to help young girls gain a sense of self-worth and confidence in taking charge and following their dreams. It was called the 'I'm not bossy, I'm a boss' campaign. That sums up her attitude. It's all about following your passions and doing things so well that nobody else can match your talent, while at the same time remaining humble and supportive of others. Beyoncé's work ethic and general attitude towards life inspires me a lot, and her music makes me feel empowered. She's a diva, but in a good way, and she owns it.

MACARONS

When making the meringue for the macarons, add the food gels at about the 3-minute mark and mix until well combined. Bake, then allow to cool.

GOLD PAINT

To prepare the gold paint, combine the gold lustre dust and vodka in a small mixing bowl and mix until well combined.

Once the macarons are baked and cooled, use a food-safe paintbrush to paint all of the macaron shells gold. Yes, this will take some time, but it's just the way it is. Throw on your favourite album or podcast and go for it! Once painted, leave the shells at room temperature to dry completely.

ASSEMBLY

Fit the end of a piping bag with a Wilton 6B tip, fill it with the ganache and pipe a swirl of ganache on the flat side of half the macaron shells, then sandwich with the remaining shells. Chill for 20 minutes, then finish off by painting the exposed ganache with more gold paint. Allow to dry.

REBELS REJOICE

Celebrate good times, c'mon!

I hope that song is stuck in your head now, ha! I love it! This collection of cupcakes is all about celebrating those good times in your life. You know, the really important ones like birthdays or Christmas, because you need something to help you get through meeting your sister's latest flame who will not shut up about his ostrich farm comeback idea. There are even Golden goose egg cupcakes for Easter (see page 198) and blood-red Cherry cherry boom boom cupcakes (see page 202) for Valentine's Day. I'm pretty sure I've hit all the important holidays in this collection.

BOOZY CHRISTMAS PUDDING *cupcakes*

EASY

MAKES **10** CUPCAKES

10 brown cupcake cases

CUPCAKES

1 batch Chocolate cupcakes (page 38)
60 ml (2 fl oz/¼ cup) Baileys or Kahlua

BOOZY CHOCOLATE SAUCE

2 tablespoons Baileys or Kahlua
1 batch Chocolate sauce (page 51)

WHITE CHOCOLATE GANACHE

200 g (7 oz) white chocolate buttons
80 ml (2½ fl oz/⅓ cup) thickened (whipping) cream

FROSTING

¾ batch chocolate-flavoured American buttercream frosting (page 45)

DECORATIONS

200 g (7 oz/1½ cups) chocolate shavings
12 Jaffas (chocolate-orange ball candies)
24 small mint leaves, to garnish

Of all the holidays in the year, Christmas is the time to be good, because the big fella is checking his list and, according to my sources, he checks that list twice. But it's OK to be a little naughty too, and these spiked Christmas cupcakes will help. You should definitely leave some out for jolly St. Nick!

CUPCAKES

When making the cupcake batter, add the Baileys with the wet ingredients. Bake, then allow to cool.

BOOZY CHOCOLATE SAUCE

While the cupcakes are cooling, add the Baileys to the chocolate sauce and mix well.

WHITE CHOCOLATE SAUCE

Prepare the white chocolate sauce by combining the white chocolate and cream in a large, microwave-safe bowl. Microwave on high, for 20 seconds at a time, mixing well between each interval until smooth. Allow the sauce to reach room temperature before using, otherwise it will be too thin to go on the cupcake.

ASSEMBLY

Core the centre of each cupcake with an apple corer (stop about 1 cm (½ in) from the bottom) and fill with boozy chocolate sauce.

Fit the end of a piping bag with a large round tip, fill with the chocolate frosting and pipe a bulb of frosting on top of each cupcake.

Next, dip the frosting into a bowl of chocolate shavings, rolling the cupcake around to achieve a nice bulb shape.

Pour some white chocolate sauce over the top, place two Jaffas in the centre and finish with two small mint leaves right before serving.

MEDIUM

MAKES **10** CUPCAKES

INSPIRED BY: **ALL I WANT FOR CHRISTMAS IS YOU – MARIAH CAREY**

10 white cupcake cases

CUPCAKES & DOUGHNUTS

1 batch Vanilla cupcakes (page 34)
4 drops red food-gel colouring
2 teaspoons peppermint extract
200 g (7 oz) mini dark chocolate chips

WHITE CHOCOLATE GANACHE

290 g (10 oz) white chocolate buttons
60 ml (2 fl oz/¼ cup) thickened (whipping) cream

FROSTING

2 teaspoons peppermint extract
1 batch Swiss meringue buttercream frosting (page 46)
4 drops red food-gel colouring

DECORATIONS

1 batch Chocolate sauce (page 51)
10 mini candy canes
10 white-chocolate ball candies

Something you guys don't know about me is that I'm not actually a fan of Christmas music. At all. As soon as November hits, I take my headphones with me wherever I go so I can drown out all the Christmas music. There's only one exception, and that's Mariah Carey's 'All I Want For Christmas Is You'. The OG Christmas diva, belting it out every Christmas. That's my idea of Christmas spirit.

CUPCAKES & DOUGHNUTS

Line a cupcake tin with the cupcake cases. Spray a doughnut tin with oil and use a paper towel to wipe away any excess. Set aside.

When making the cupcake batter, add the red food gel and peppermint extract with the wet ingredients.

Add the mini chocolate chips to the bottom of the doughnut tin and pipe the batter on top. Fill the moulds just above halfway.

Fill each cupcake case three-quarters of the way. Bake the doughnuts for 15 minutes and the cupcakes for 40 minutes. Allow the cupcakes to cool.

To get the doughnuts out of the hot doughnut tin, place a wire rack directly on top of the tin. Grip the tin and the rack with two tea towels (dish towels) and flip the tin over. Gently tap the base of the doughnut tin. This will allow the doughnuts to fall out easily without them ripping. It's best to do this as soon as they come out of the oven to stop them from cooking any further as the tin cools.

WHITE CHOCOLATE GANACHE

Combine the white chocolate and cream in a microwave-safe bowl and microwave on high, for 20 seconds at a time, mixing well between each interval until smooth. Set aside at room temperature to cool before using.

FROSTING

Add the peppermint extract to the frosting and mix until well combined. Set aside one-quarter of the frosting in a bowl, add the red food gel and mix until well combined. Transfer the frostings to separate piping bags and snip off the ends.

Lay out a sheet of plastic wrap on your work bench and pipe long lines of each frosting, alternating between red and white. Use the plastic wrap to help you roll up the frosting like a sushi roll into a log shape, then twist each end to secure. Snip off one end of the log and place it, cut side down, inside a piping bag fitted with a medium round tip.

ASSEMBLY

Core each cupcake with an apple corer (stop about 1 cm (½ in) from the bottom) and fill with chocolate sauce. Frost a double-doughnut swirl (see page 14) on top and drizzle with more chocolate sauce. Push a doughnut into the frosting, upright, and drizzle with white ganache. Add two candy canes and finish with a white-chocolate ball candy.

CHEESECAKE EASTER-EGG HUNT *cupcakes*

HARD

MAKES 10 CUPCAKES

10 white cupcake cases

CHEESECAKE FILLING

250 g (9 oz) cream cheese, at room temperature
175 ml (6 fl oz) sweetened condensed milk
1 teaspoon vanilla extract

EGG-YOLK CURD

1 drop orange food-gel colouring
1 drop yellow food-gel colouring
200 g (7 oz) lemon curd

CUPCAKES

1 batch Chocolate cupcakes (page 38)

SPECKLED EGGS

340 g (12 oz) Wilton turquoise candy melts, melted
340 g (12 oz) Wilton white candy melts, melted
200 g (7 oz) crushed Oreos

DECORATIONS

300 g (10½ oz) mini speckled Easter eggs
crushed coloured sprinkles
small mint leaves, to garnish

FROSTING

1 batch Chocolate ganache frosting (page 49)

One of my earliest memories as a kid was dyeing Easter eggs red for Greek Easter with my mum and yiayia. It was a challenge every year to see if we could make them without them cracking. And then, of course, comes the game of cracking them against one another's chosen Easter eggs. If, at the end, your egg hadn't cracked, you were the winner. The winner of what, though? I still don't know. My cousin put his in the freezer one year and beat everyone.

CHEESECAKE FILLING

Add the cream cheese to a large mixing bowl with the sweetened condensed milk and vanilla. Use a hand mixer to beat the mixture until creamy. Cover with plastic wrap and set aside.

EGG-YOLK CURD

Add the food gels to the lemon curd and mix until well combined.

CUPCAKES

Prepare the chocolate cupcakes. Bake, then allow to cool.

SPECKLED EGGS

For this recipe, you will need a silicone 10- or 12-egg Easter-egg mould about the size of an actual egg (they are available online). You will need to repeat the below steps until you have created 20 egg halves, or you can use two egg moulds.

Melt the turquoise and white candy melts separately, then combine once melted.

Wipe the inside of your Easter-egg mould using a damp paper towel. Scatter over 2 teaspoons of the crushed Oreos, making sure the moulds are well covered, then tap to remove any excess. This will create your speckled-egg effect. Add 1 teaspoon of the melted candy and, using the back of a teaspoon, carefully spread it evenly around the mould, making sure it comes up just over the edge. Use a small offset spatula to scrape any excess candy from the surface of the mould to create an even, straight top. Flush, clean edges will ensure that your egg halves join neatly later. Chill for 20 minutes.

Once the candy shells have chilled, pipe the cream cheese mixture into the moulds, filling them up just under halfway. Use the back of a teaspoon to create an indent in the cream cheese about the size of an egg yolk, then pipe a blob of lemon curd in the centre. Again, make sure you don't overfill your moulds. Chill for 1 hour.

Carefully remove the filled egg halves from the mould and use a toothpick to smear some melted chocolate around the edges of half of them. Stick two halves together to create full eggs. Use your finger to wipe away any excess melted chocolate.

To work on your eggs, place them in a hard boiled egg holder, or rest them inside a small round cookie cutter. Run a sharp knife under hot water and dry with a paper towel. Carefully cut out some zig-zag shapes from the top of your eggs to make them appear as if a cute little bird has chipped its way out. This process can be a little messy because the eggs are filled with cheesecake, but just persevere and wipe away any excess filling as you go.

Add an extra dab of lemon curd on top to look like runny egg yolk.

ASSEMBLY

Core the centre of each cupcake with an apple corer (stop about 1 cm (½ in) from the bottom) and fill with as many mini speckled eggs as you can.

Fit the end of a piping bag with a Wilton #4 tip, fill with ganache and pipe some ganache around the mini eggs, using the back of a teaspoon to level it at the top. Sprinkle with some crushed Oreos and pat down with the teaspoon.

To make the bird's nest, pipe some more chocolate ganache in U-shapes around the edge of the cupcake. Start in the centre, work towards the outside of the cupcake, then back towards the middle. Continue piping until it resembles a bird's nest.

Place the speckled cheesecake eggs in the middle of the nests and finish off by decorating the birds' nests with crushed coloured sprinkles and mint leaves.

See image on page 196.

CHEESECAKE EASTER-EGG HUNT *cupcakes*

GOLDEN GOOSE-EGG *cupcakes*

GOLDEN GOOSE-EGG *cupcakes*

HARD

MAKES **10** CUPCAKES

10 gold-foil cupcake cases

EGGS

400 g (14 oz) dark chocolate, melted

FROSTING

2 batches Chocolate ganache frosting (page 49), softened

CUPCAKES

1 batch Chocolate cupcakes (page 38)
40 mini speckled Easter eggs

DECORATIONS

12 Ferrero Rocher chocolates

GOLD PAINT

2 teaspoons gold lustre dust
2 teaspoons vodka or vanilla extract

For these cupcakes, you'll need to find golden-goose eggs. They're quite rare. The last time anyone saw one was in Willy Wonka's factory ...

EGGS

For this recipe, you'll need a silicone 10- or 12-egg Easter-egg mould about the size of an actual egg (they are available online). You will need to repeat the below steps until you have created 20 egg halves, or you can use two egg moulds.

Fill the egg mould with the melted chocolate and give it a slight jiggle to get rid of any air bubbles. Turn it upside-down over a baking tray and allow the excess chocolate to drip out. Scrape any excess chocolate from the surface of the mould to ensure the egg halves have nice, clean edges. Leave to set in the fridge. You can use the leftover chocolate to make more eggs, or store it in a zip-lock bag at room temperature and use it in other recipes.

Once the chocolate egg halves have set, fill them about halfway with softened ganache. Place a Ferrero Rocher chocolate in one half of the egg halves and leave them to set at room temperature for 1 hour.

Carefully remove the filled egg halves from the mould and use a toothpick to smear some melted chocolate around the edges of half of them. Stick two halves together, to create full eggs. Use your finger to wipe away any excess melted chocolate. Don't worry too much about finger marks, because you'll be painting over them. Refrigerate for 1 hour to set.

CUPCAKES

Once the cupcake batter is ready, fold in the speckled eggs. Bake, then allow to cool.

FROSTING

For the frosting, first make sure that your ganache is soft enough to pipe, but firm enough to hold its shape. If it's too stiff, you can soften your ganache by microwaving it on high for 10 seconds, mixing, then microwaving again, for 5 seconds at a time, until it's soft enough.

ASSEMBLY

Fit the end of a piping bag with a round tip, fill with the ganache and pipe a bulb of ganache on top of each cupcake. Nestle a chocolate egg on top.

Fit the end of another piping bag with a Wilton #125 petal tip.

Place a rubber grip mat on a cake turntable and sit your cupcake on top.

Make sure the widest part of the petal tip is facing down when you pipe around the cupcake. Start at the base of the cupcake and use the turntable to spin the cupcake as you pipe, making your way to just above the base of the egg. Repeat with the remaining cupcakes, then chill for 1 hour to allow the ganache to firm up before you paint it.

GOLD PAINT

To make the gold paint, mix the gold lustre dust and vodka together in a small bowl. Use a food-safe paintbrush to paint the ganache and the egg. You may need to use two coats of paint on the egg. Let the first coat dry before adding the second coat.

See image on page 197.

SPECKLED EGG *macarons*

EASY

MAKES 15 SANDWICHED MACARONS

One of my favourite things about Easter is chocolate. I mean, I'm an adult now, so I can stay up as late as I want and eat as much chocolate as I like, right? No. I'm a curvy woman now, and if I get any curvier then I'm gonna need a crane to remove me from my house. But Easter is the perfect time of year to have a cheeky helping of chocolate. My favourite choccy eggs are the speckled ones – they're so pretty! So, here's my version of it in a macaron.

FROSTING

2 teaspoons strawberry flavouring
1 drop pink food-gel colouring
1 batch Swiss meringue buttercream frosting (page 46)

MACARONS

1 batch Vanilla macarons (page 42)
1 drop sky-blue food-gel colouring
3 drops teal food-gel colouring

CHOCOLATE SPLATTER

3 tablespoons sifted unsweetened (Dutch) cocoa powder
2 tablespoons boiling water

DECORATIONS

500 g (1 lb 2 oz) mini speckled Easter eggs

FROSTING

Add the strawberry flavouring and pink food gel to the frosting and mix until well combined.

MACARONS

When making the meringue for the macarons, add the food gels at about the 3-minute mark and mix until well combined.

When piping the macarons, pipe them 5 cm (2 in) in diameter. Allow to dry, then bake.

CHOCOLATE SPLATTER

To prepare the chocolate splatter, combine the sifted cocoa powder and boiling water in a bowl and mix until the cocoa powder has dissolved. It should be thin enough to splatter.

Once the macarons have cooled, dip a BRAND-NEW TOOTHBRUSH (brand new, people; these aren't supposed to be toothpaste-flavoured macarons) into the chocolate splatter and run your finger along the bristles to splatter it onto the macaron shells. (Also, don't wear a white t-shirt while you're doing this.) Leave them to dry for 30 minutes before handling them.

ASSEMBLY

Fit the end of a piping bag with a round tip, fill with the frosting and pipe a blob of frosting on the flat side of half the macaron shells. You're going to use the frosting to help stand the eggs up. Add the mini eggs in a ring around the outer edge of the frosting, then sandwich with the remaining shells.

CHERRY CHERRY BOOM BOOM *cupcakes*

EASY

MAKES 20 CUPCAKES

INSPIRED BY: EH EH THERE'S NOTHING ELSE I CAN SAY – LADY GAGA

20 white cupcake cases

CHERRY FILLING

115 g (4 oz/½ cup, firmly packed) brown sugar
2 tablespoons cornflour (cornstarch) mixed with 3 tablespoons water
1 pinch fine salt
600 g (1 lb 5 oz/3 cups) tinned whole pitted cherries, drained (reserve 200 ml (7 fl oz) of the cherry juice)
½ teaspoon vanilla extract

CUPCAKES

1 batch Vanilla cupcakes (page 34)
6–10 drops red food-gel colouring
1 teaspoon unsweetened (Dutch) cocoa powder
125 ml (4 fl oz/½ cup) cherry liqueur

FROSTING

6–10 drops red food-gel colouring
1 teaspoon unsweetened (Dutch) cocoa powder
125 ml (4 fl oz/½ cup) cherry liqueur
1 batch American buttercream frosting (page 45)

DECORATIONS

20 maraschino cherries, well drained

Yet another Gaga-inspired cupcake! This one is all about cherries. I took inspiration from a lyric in a Gaga song, which ended up being the title of the cupcake. I also really wanted to pack a punch with flavour, so if you love cherries then this one is for you!

CHERRY FILLING

Place the sugar, cornflour and salt in a saucepan and mix until well combined. Add the cherries, along with the cherry juice. Place over a medium heat and stir until the mixture begins to thicken. Transfer to a bowl, cover with plastic wrap and allow to cool.

CUPCAKES

Add the red food gel, cocoa powder and cherry liqueur with the wet ingredients. Bake, then allow to cool.

FROSTING

Add the red food gel, cocoa powder and cherry liqueur to the frosting and mix until well combined.

ASSEMBLY

Core the centre of each cupcake with an apple corer (stop about 1 cm (½ in) from the bottom) and fill with the cooled cherry filling.

Fit the end of a piping bag with a Wilton 1M tip, fill with the frosting and pipe a signature swirl of frosting (page 14) on top of each cupcake. Finish off with a maraschino cherry.

HARD

MAKES 10 CUPCAKES

10 white cupcake cases

CHEESECAKE LAYERS

5 teaspoons powdered gelatin
400 ml (13½ fl oz) sweetened condensed milk
500 g (1 lb 2 oz) full-fat cream cheese
1 teaspoon vanilla extract

CUPCAKES

5 drops bright-white food-gel colouring
½ batch Vanilla cupcakes (page 34)

MIRROR GLAZE

19 g (¾ oz) powdered gelatin
200 ml (7 fl oz) sweetened condensed milk
300 g (10½ oz) granulated sugar
350 g (12½ oz) white chocolate chips
10 drops bright-white food-gel colouring

DECORATIONS

10 white sugar flowers
185 g (6½ oz/1 cup) white soft sugar pearls

Can you imagine how cute these would look at your first wedding? And your second and third? Your guests would love having these sitting at their table. I know I would!

CHEESECAKE LAYERS

Spray a 30 × 20 cm (12 × 8 in) rectangular baking tin with oil and line with baking paper. Set aside.

Add the gelatin and 125 ml (4 fl oz/½ cup) water to a microwave-safe bowl. Mix until well combined and allow to sit for 5 minutes, then microwave on high for 10 seconds.

Add the sweetened condensed milk to another microwave-safe bowl and microwave on high for 1 minute. Add the melted gelatin mixture and mix until well combined.

Put the cream cheese in a large mixing bowl and beat with a hand mixer until smooth. Add the milk-and-gelatin mixture and vanilla, and mix again until smooth.

Pour the mixture into the prepared baking tin and smooth it out using a large spatula. Cover with plastic wrap and chill for 2–3 hours, or overnight.

You'll need three different-sized round cookie cutters to make the three layers. The biggest should be the same size as the top of your cupcakes; the middle a little smaller, and the top, smaller again. Cut out ten rounds of cheesecake with each of the three cutters. Once you have all your rounds cut out, set them aside on a baking tray lined with baking paper and cover with plastic wrap until you're ready to decorate with the mirror glaze.

CUPCAKES

Add the food gel to the cupcake batter with the wet ingredients. Bake, then allow to cool.

MIRROR GLAZE

Combine the gelatin with 125 ml (4 fl oz/½ cup) water in a small mixing bowl and set aside for 5 minutes.

Combine the milk, sugar and 150 ml (5 fl oz) water in a saucepan over a medium heat and bring to a simmer. Add the gelatin mixture and stir until dissolved.

Place the chocolate chips in a large, heatproof bowl. Pour the hot milk mixture over the chocolate and let it sit for 5 minutes. Once the chocolate has softened, use a hand-held blender to blitz the mixture until smooth. Add the bright-white food gel and mix until well combined, then pass the mixture through a fine-mesh sieve to remove any remaining lumps.

Allow the glaze to cool to 33°C (91°F) before using.

ASSEMBLY

To finish off your cupcakes, stack the three different-sized cheesecake layers on top of each other, then set the stacks on a wire rack set over a baking tray. Pour the mirror glaze over the top and leave them to set for 10–20 minutes before carefully placing them on top of your cupcakes.

Add sugar flowers to the top of the cheesecake stacks and decorate the bases with sugar pearls.

NO-BAKE BIRTHDAY CAKE *cupcakes*

EASY

MAKES **10** CUPCAKES

10 silver-foil cupcake cases

CUPCAKES

1 batch Chocolate cupcakes (page 38)

FROSTING

1 batch Swiss meringue buttercream frosting (page 46)

DECORATIONS

185 g (6½ oz/1 cup) confetti sprinkles

Yes, there is a way to make cupcakes without an oven! I only recently discovered this technique. It's amazing and the cupcakes come out just as moist.

CUPCAKES

For this recipe, you'll need a four-hole silicone cupcake tray. Make sure that it is small enough to fit inside a deep frying pan with the lid on top. Line the tray with four cupcake cases.

Lay a large tea towel (dish towel) on your work bench and use it to wrap the lid of your frying pan. Tie it at the top with an elastic band. Make sure it is securely tied to prevent it falling off during the cooking time. This is especially important if you are using a gas stove.

Make the cupcake batter and fill each cupcake case about three-quarters of the way.

Place the silicone tray in the frying pan. Fill the pan with enough water to come about halfway up the side of the tray.

Cover with the lid and cook over a medium heat on the stovetop for 40 minutes. Once cooked, take the tray out of the pan and leave the cupcakes to cool completely. Repeat with the remaining cupcake batter to make ten cupcakes.

ASSEMBLY

Fit the end of a piping bag with a Wilton 6B tip, fill with the frosting and pipe a swirl of frosting on top of each cupcake. Sprinkle with confetti sprinkles.

STRAWBERRY BIRTHDAY *cake*

HARD

SERVES **30**

CRUMB-COAT FROSTING

2 teaspoons strawberry flavouring
2 batches Swiss meringue buttercream frosting (page 46)

STRIPED FROSTING

2 teaspoons strawberry flavouring
2 batches Swiss meringue buttercream frosting (page 46)
light pink: 3 drops pink food-gel colouring and 2 drops strawberry flavouring
dark pink: 4 drops pink food-gel colouring and 2 drops strawberry flavouring

CAKE

2 batches Vanilla cake (page 37)
315 g (11 oz/1 cup) strawberry jam
1 teaspoon strawberry flavouring
2 drops pink food-gel colouring
185 g (6½ oz/1 cup) rainbow confetti sprinkles, plus extra to sprinkle between the cake layers

DECORATIONS

185 g (6½ oz/1 cup) rainbow confetti sprinkles and rainbow jimmies
12 maraschino cherries, well drained

Just pretty pink stripes and lots of sprinkles. What more could you want from a birthday cake? The answer is: nothing. This is the perfect cake for celebrating anyone's birthday: boy, girl, young, old – anyone!

CRUMB-COAT FROSTING

Add the strawberry flavouring to the frosting and mix until well combined. This is the frosting you'll use to fill and crumb-coat the cake.

STRIPED FROSTING

Add the strawberry flavouring to the frosting, then divide it between two bowls. Colour one light pink and the other dark pink using the colour formulations in the ingredients list.

CAKE

Once the batter is ready, divide it between two mixing bowls.

Add the strawberry jam, strawberry flavouring and pink food gel to one half of the batter and mix until well combined.

Add the sprinkles to the other half and fold in until just mixed. Don't overmix, because you'll risk the colours bleeding into the batter.

Transfer the batters to separate piping bags and add random blobs of batter to your three prepared cake tins until all the batter has been used. Try to fill them as evenly as you can.

Bake for 50–60 minutes, or until a toothpick inserted in the centre of a cake comes out clean. Allow the cakes to cool in their tins for 2 minutes, then carefully flip them out onto wire racks. Leave to cool completely before using.

Trim, fill and crumb-coat the cakes (see page 10) using the crumb-coat frosting. Chill for 2 hours.

To frost the striped layers, fit the ends of two piping bags with round tips. Add the light frosting to one and the dark to the other.

Pipe around the cake, alternating between the two pinks starting at the bottom and working your way towards the top. Frost the top of the cake the same colour as your last layer.

Use an offset spatula to smooth out the frosting on the top. It doesn't have to be perfect, but try to get it as level as you can. Use a cake scraper (see page 26) to smooth out the frosting on the sides until it's nice and even. Take care to hold the scraper steady as you move around the cake to ensure the colours don't blend. Once the sides are smooth, use the scraper to smooth out the top once more.

TO DECORATE

Add the sprinkles to the side of the cake, starting at the bottom and using fewer as you work your way towards the top to create an ombre effect.

Fit the end of a piping bag with a large, open-star tip, fill with the reserved plain frosting and pipe swirls of frosting on top of the cake. Sprinkle some confetti sprinkles on top.

Finish with the maraschino cherries.

See image on page 210.

STRAWBERRY BIRTHDAY *cake*

SCHOOLIN' LIFE *cake*

EASY

SERVES **30**

INSPIRED BY: **SCHOOLIN' LIFE – BEYONCÉ**

CRUMB-COAT FROSTING

2 teaspoons raspberry flavouring
2 batches Swiss meringue buttercream frosting (page 46)

OMBRE FROSTING

2 teaspoons raspberry flavouring
2 batches Swiss meringue buttercream frosting (page 46)
blue: 5 drops blue food-gel colouring and 2 drops teal food-gel colouring
medium blue: 4 drops blue food-gel colouring and 3 drops purple food-gel colouring
dark blue: 8 drops blue food-gel colouring and 8 drops purple food-gel colouring
blue-purple: 8 drops purple food-gel colouring and 4 drops blue food-gel colouring
dark purple: 8 drops purple food-gel colouring and 2 drops blue food-gel colouring
purple: 8 drops purple food-gel colouring and 4 pink purple food-gel colouring

This story has a happy ending, I promise. So, I have this thing where I don't really like celebrating my birthday. Part of the reason is (and I never thought I'd become one of these people) that I don't like getting older. I had good birthdays when I was a kid, but the worst birthday I ever had was when I turned 30. Oh lawd. I was not having it. I went into full mourning mode. I literally locked myself in my room and sulked all day because I wasn't in my 20s anymore.

Guess what? My 30s have been the best years of my life. I'm doing all these things I never thought I would ever do. Sure, I'm not as skinny as I was in my 20s, but I've become a confident person who knows who he is and is living his best life. My 20s were just me finding who I was, but I didn't realise that at the time. I still feel young. I'm just more grown up in my mind.

Beyoncé has a song called Schoolin' Life that's about celebrating your age, who you are and living your best life. I love it. It's got this awesome '80s vibe. So, this cake is for everyone at any age.

CRUMB-COAT FROSTING

Add the raspberry flavouring to the frosting and mix until well combined.

OMBRE FROSTING

Add the raspberry flavouring to the frosting and mix until well combined. Divide the frosting between six small bowls and colour each one separately following the colour formulations in the ingredients list. Transfer the coloured frostings to separate piping bags and snip about 2 cm (¾ in) off the end of each bag.

SILVER PAINT

Combine the silver lustre dust and vodka in a small bowl and mix until well combined. Set aside.

RASPBERRY GANACHE

Combine the pink candy melts, cream and raspberry flavouring in a microwave-safe bowl. Microwave on high, for 20 seconds at a time, mixing between each interval until smooth. Leave to sit at room temperature to set a little before you use it.

SILVER PAINT

3 tablespoons silver lustre dust
3 tablespoons vodka or vanilla extract

RASPBERRY GANACHE

300 g (10½ oz) Wilton pink candy melts
100 ml (3½ oz) thickened (whipping) cream
2 teaspoons raspberry flavouring

CAKE

2 batches Vanilla cake (page 37)
2 teaspoons raspberry flavouring
5 drops blue food-gel colouring
5 drops pink food-gel colouring

DECORATIONS

185 g (6½ oz/1 cup) rainbow confetti sprinkles

CAKE

Add the raspberry flavouring with the wet ingredients.

Divide the batter between two mixing bowls. Colour one blue and the other pink. Transfer the batters to separate piping bags and pipe squiggles of each colour into your three prepared cake tins. Bake, then chill.

Trim, fill and crumb-coat your cake (see page 10) using the crumb-coat frosting, then chill for 2 hours.

To create the ombre frosting, begin by piping a line of blue frosting at the bottom of the cake, followed by the medium blue, dark blue, blue-purple and dark purple, then finish with the purple frosting. Top the cake with more purple frosting.

Use a small offset spatula to smooth out the frosting on the top of the cake. Don't worry about making it perfectly smooth, because we're going to come back to it.

Use a cake scraper (see page 26) to smooth out the frosting around the cake. Scrape the frosting off the cake scraper as you go to keep the ombre looking nice and neat. Use the scraper to smooth out the top of the cake.

TO DECORATE

Flick silver paint onto the sides of the cake using a food-safe paintbrush. Next, add confetti sprinkles, starting with a heavier layer at the bottom, then using fewer as you work your way towards the top.

Drizzle the top of the cake with raspberry ganache.

To prepare the swirls on top, lay out a large sheet of plastic wrap on your work bench and pipe long lines of each coloured frosting. Use the plastic wrap to help you roll up the frosting like a sushi roll into a log shape, then twist each end to secure. Snip off one end of the log and place it, cut side down, inside a piping bag fitted with a Wilton 1M tip.

Pipe swirls of rainbow frosting on top of the cake.

See image on page 211.

HEY NICK,

I get loads of emails and questions in the comments section of my posts, and I do my best to answer as many of them as I can. Here's a list of the most common questions you guys ask and some funny ones that I wanted to include for a laugh.

You can always ask me questions through my website, www.thescranline.com, or on social media :)

BAKING QUESTIONS CONTINUED

Can I replace the sugar in your frosting recipe with flour? I don't like things that are too sweet.

I've legit been asked this question more than once. Here's my answer:

You could ... though if you add eggs, you're halfway to making a cake.

How do you get your cake frosting so smooth? Do you freeze the cakes first, or is there another tactic to get a smooth frosting layer without the cake crumbling into it?

So, first of all, make sure you crumb-coat your cakes (see page 10). I also use Swiss meringue buttercream frosting for my cakes because it goes on a lot smoother and shinier than American buttercream. To get them super smooth, I then use a cake scraper (see page 26).

Should I add more milk powder to the cream cheese frosting to make it stiffer? I live in a very hot and humid country.

You can, but if it's hot, then there's not much you can do to keep frosting stiff. This is what I do on hot days with any frosting: turn the aircon on two hours before I start using the kitchen, so the kitchen is as cool as possible when I start. I also keep my cakes and cupcakes chilled up until about 30 minutes before I serve them. On hot days, it doesn't take long for them to come to room temperature.

How can I replace the eggs in your cake recipes?

You can't. I think it's better to find a recipe that has been designed not to have eggs in it. Once you start taking out or replacing ingredients in a cake recipe, you risk getting different results.

What can I do with leftover frosting or sauce?

Chocolate and caramel sauce can be stored in an airtight container in the fridge for months. Frosting can be stored in an airtight container for up to one week. The problem with frosting is that it's porous, so it can take on fridge smells very easily. Soften your frosting in the microwave for 10 seconds at a time before whipping again to reuse.

How do you keep two, or three (or more) layered, iced cakes moist and fresh in the fridge? Mine become so hard!

OK, so kudos to you for having enough space in your fridge for a three-tiered cake. When you make cakes, you should crumb-coat them. It helps trap the crumbs in the first layer of frosting, but it also helps to seal the cake and protects it from drying out. So, if you crumb-coat your cakes, they shouldn't dry out.

MACARON QUESTIONS

What's the difference between a macaron and a macaroon?

A macaroon is a coconut cookie, and a macaron is the French cookie made of almond flour and egg whites.

I love macarons, but they're always so sweet. Do you have any recipes for macarons, or even just fillings, that aren't as sweet and overpowering?

Sugar plays several roles in a dessert. Yes, it makes a dessert sweet, but sugar also helps a cake rise. Try making a cake without sugar and see what happens. I've done it. Apart from not being sweet at all, the cake is dense and gross. You can't mess around with the ingredients in a cake or a macaron unfortunately, but you can help cut the sweetness with a tart berry or fruit filling.

Have you ever thought about making macarons using the French method?

I have made macarons using the French method. Back when I was learning to make macarons, I tried both the Italian-meringue method and the French method (see page 42) and I found the Italian-meringue method resulted in much more consistently good macarons.

Is there a way to make macarons almond-free for people with allergies?

There is, but as of right now, I've never tried it.

What is a good alternative if you don't have a silicone baking mat/sheet for macarons?

Baking paper! Don't confuse that with greaseproof paper.

Do you think the weather (e.g. humidity) can affect how your macarons turn out?

Yes! It definitely can. Specifically, when it comes to how long your macarons need to dry.

Have you ever tried making vegan macarons?

About five times, but not successfully – yet.

I am mesmerised by your macaron recipes! I was wondering if you could give the approximate number of strokes required to reach the right consistency for the 'macaronage' step?

It's less about how many times you mix the batter and more about getting the right consistency (see page 18).

I live in Florida where it is always extremely humid and even after setting my macarons out for at least an hour, they never seem to form a skin. Is there anything I can do about this?

Yeah actually, I've found that having the fan on or your aircon will make them dry out a lot quicker. Don't put them directly under the fan or aircon, but just having air circulate in the room will help to dry them out enough before you bake them.

Can I make your macaron recipe without a sugar thermometer? And, if I can, over what heat should I boil the sugar and the water, and for how many minutes?

You can, but I'm not even going to try to explain it because it's easier to hand over your $20 and buy a sugar thermometer. It takes out all the guesswork. Without a sugar thermometer, you will have to guess what the temperature of your syrup is, which is too risky.

SOME MORE NICK QUESTIONS

Do you ever wish you had a different job?

No. I don't wish I had a different job right now, but I see my job evolving and changing in the future. I'm not sure how yet.

If you could meet one person, alive or dead, who would it be and what would you bake them?

My Yiayia. I would give up The Scran Line to sit with her in her kitchen listening to her stories again. I would bake her some macarons. She loved them.

What's your ethnicity/first language?

I'm Australian with Greek heritage. I speak English and Greek.

Where do you see yourself in five years?

In my 32 years on this planet, I've learned not to plan too far ahead. It just doesn't work for me; something completely different always happens. Three years ago, I didn't think I'd be making a book. It wasn't something I planned, but I was very lucky to be offered the opportunity and I took it!

INDEX

A
activated charcoal 163
almond flour vs almond meal 18
almond meal 18
American buttercream frosting 45
  tips and tricks 12
Aussie gold macarons 110

B
baking
  baking questions 163, 214
  baking times 10
  tips and tricks 9
  tools and equipment 21–9
  utensils 25, 29, 163
Banana cake 144–5
Banana doughnuts 144–5
Banana hammock freakshake cake 144–5
Birthday cake macarons 104
Black frosting 66–7, 124–5
Black velvet cupcakes 66–7
Black-velvet crumb 66–7
Blood syrup 119
Bloody syrup 122–3
Boozy chocolate sauce 191
Boozy Christmas pudding cupcakes 191
Brain food cupcakes 115
Brain worms 115
Bubblegum goo 56–7
Bubblepop electric cupcakes 56–7
bubbles, Pink gelatin 56–7
butter, softening 9
buttercream, Molasses 96–7

C
Cactus decorations 98–9
Cactus garden cake 98–9
cakes
  Banana hammock freakshake cake 144–5
  Cactus garden cake 98–9
  Celebrate good times cake 158–9
  Chocolate cake 41
  cutting 16
  decorating 26
  Double-stack Oreo cake 92–3
  Giant funfetti cookie dough cake 96–7
  Highway unicorn cake 70–1
  Lemonade cake 181
  Magic mushroom cake 102–103
  preparing cake tins 10
  Schoolin' life cake 212–3
  Strawberry birthday cake 208–9
  tips and tricks 9
  Vanilla cake 37
  Vegan chocolate raspberry cake 78–9
  Voodoo Halloween cake 124–5
cameras 26
Candy cane freakshake cupcakes 192
Candy shards 116–17, 154, 172–3, 178
Candy spikes 121
Cat eyes 156
Catching feelings macarons 183
Celebrate good times cake 158–9
Cheesecake Easter-egg hunt cupcakes 194–5
Cherry cherry boom boom cupcakes 202
Cherry filling 202
Chic freak cupcakes 121
Choc cherry cola cupcakes 138
Chocolate bark 102–3
chocolate bars, Mini 140–1
Chocolate cake 41
Chocolate cupcakes 38
Chocolate ganache 144–5
Chocolate ganache frosting 49
Chocolate paint 72
Chocolate sauce 51, 138
Chocolate skull 124–5
Chocolate splatter 201
Choux pastry 83–4
Coffee mixture 91
coming out 148
Cookie dough 96–7
cookies, Peach 64–5
Cream cheese frosting 47
  tips and tricks 12
Cream topping 82
creaming method 34
Crème pâtissière 83
crumb-coating 10
crumb, Black-velvet 66–7
Cube cakes 66–7
cupcakes
  Black velvet cupcakes 66–7
  Boozy Christmas pudding cupcakes 191
  Brain food cupcakes 115
  Bubblepop electric cupcakes 56–7
  Candy cane freakshake cupcakes 192
  Cheesecake Easter-egg hunt cupcakes 194–5
  Cherry cherry boom boom cupcakes 202
  Chic freak cupcakes 121
  Choc cherry cola cupcakes 138
  Chocolate cupcakes 38
  creaming method 34
  Dancing queen cupcakes 151
  Dead velvet cupcakes 119
  Diamond heart cupcakes 172–3
  Femme queen realness – the realness cupcakes 154
  Freakfetti cupcakes 140–1
  Friend of Dorothy cupcakes 153
  Galaxy space time cupcakes 174
  Get in to the groove cupcakes 168–9
  Golden goose-egg cupcakes 198–9
  Good witch, bad bish cupcakes 116–17
  In his kiss cupcakes 178
  Kitty girl cupcakes 156
  Midnight galaxy cupcakes 61
  Mint choc-chip freakshake cupcakes 130–1
  Neapolitan cupcakes 89
  No-bake birthday cake cupcakes 207
  Paris brest cupcakes 83–4
  Peach bum cupcakes 64–5
  Platinum blonde cupcakes 177
  Red velvet cupcakes 33
  reverse-creaming method 34
  Salted caramel cupcakes 86
  Sea Kween cupcakes 58
  Silicone daydream cupcakes 122–3
  Speckled egg macarons cupcakes 201
  Sugar-free mint mocha milkshake cupcakes 136–7
  Sundae fundae cupcakes 62–3
  tips and tricks 9
  Tiramisu cupcakes 91
  Vanilla cupcakes 34
  Vegan cookies and cream cupcakes 77
  Watermelon freakshake cupcakes 134–5
  Wedding cake cupcakes 204–5
  When macaron met cupcake cupcakes 82

D
Dancing queen cupcakes 151
Dead velvet cupcakes 119

decorations
- Black-velvet crumb 66–7
- Blood syrup 119
- Bloody syrup 122–3
- Brain worms 115
- Bubblegum goo 56–7
- Cactus decorations 98–9
- Candy shards 116–17, 154, 172–3, 178
- Candy spikes 121
- Cat eyes 156
- Chocolate bark 102–3
- Chocolate paint 72
- Chocolate skull 124–5
- Chocolate splatter 201
- Cube cakes 66–7
- decorating cakes 26
- drips, making 16
- Eggs (chocolate) 194–5, 198–9, 201
- Flowers 102–3
- frosting styles 14
- Gold drip 71
- Gold drizzle 58
- Gold paint 124–5, 186, 198–9, 212–3
- Groovy decorations 168
- Highway unicorn macarons 71
- Jelly jewels 181
- Magic mushrooms 102–3
- Mini chocolate bars 140–1
- Peach cookies 64–5
- Pink gelatin bubbles 56–7
- Pink princess crowns 154
- Silver-star splatter 61
- Speckled eggs 194–5
- Teal ganache drizzle 98–9
- White chocolate spheres 158–9

Diamond heart cupcakes 172–3
Divas getting money macarons 186
double-doughnut swirl frosting 14
Double-stack Oreo cake 92–3
doughnuts
- Banana doughnuts 144–5
- Freakfetti doughnuts 140–1
- Mint choc-chip freakshake doughnuts 130–1
- Watermelon freakshake doughnuts 134–5

drips, how to create 16
drizzle, Gold 58
drizzle, Teal ganache 98–9

E

Egg yolk curd 194–5
eggs
- ageing 18
- carton 18
- replacements 215

Eggs (chocolate) 194–5, 198–9, 201

F

FAQs 52–3, 163, 214–5
Femme queen realness – the realness cupcakes 154
filling a cake 10
Flowers 102–3
food colouring 163
food processors 21
Forbidden doughnut macarons 106–107
Freakfetti cupcakes 140–1
Friend of Dorothy cupcakes 153
frosting 12–13, 56–7, 58, 61, 62–3, 66–7, 70–1, 86, 89, 91, 92–3, 104, 106–7, 109, 110, 115, 116–17, 119, 121, 122–3, 126, 134–5, 138, 151, 159, 162, 168, 172–3, 174, 177, 178, 181, 183, 192, 201, 202
- American buttercream frosting 45
- Black frosting 66–7, 124–5
- Chocolate ganache frosting 49
- Coloured frosting 156
- Cream cheese frosting 47
- Crumb-coat frosting 144–5, 208–9, 212–13
- double-doughnut swirl style 14
- frosting a cake 12
- frosting styles 14
- Grass frosting 102–3
- leftovers 214
- Ombre frosting 212–13
- Pink frosting 156
- Rainbow frosting 153
- Raspberry frosting 98–9
- Red frosting 153
- round bulb style 14
- Royal icing 107–7
- signature swirl style 14
- soft-serve swirl style 14
- Strawberry frosting 96–7
- Striped frosting 98–9, 208–9
- Sugar-free buttercream frosting 136–7
- Swiss meringue buttercream frosting 46
- tips and tricks 10, 12–13, 14, 214
- Vegan buttercream frosting 48
- Vegan chocolate frosting 78–9
- Vegan frosting 77
- White frosting 124–5

G

Galaxy space time cupcakes 174
ganache 62–3, 64–5, 116–17
- Chocolate ganache 144–5
- Green ganache 134–5
- Raspberry ganache 212–13
- Strawberry ganache 140–1
- Teal ganache drizzle 98–9
- White chocolate ganache 192

Get in to the groove cupcakes 168–9
Giant funfetti cookie dough cake 96–7
glazes
- Mirror glaze 172–3, 204
- Skin mirror glaze 122–3

Gold drip 71
Gold paint 124–5, 186, 198–9, 212–13
Golden goose-egg cupcakes 198–9
goo, Bubblegum 56–7
Good witch, bad bish cupcakes 116–17
Grass frosting 102–3
Green ganache 134–5
Groovy decorations 168

H

hand mixer 9, 21
Hey Nick 52–3, 163, 214–5
Highway unicorn cake 70–1
Highway unicorn macarons 71
how to create drips 16
how to cut cake 16
how to pipe like a pro 13
how to use this book 6
humidity 215

I

Ice cream 72
ice-cream scoops 22, 163
icing, Royal 106–7
In his kiss cupcakes 178
inspiration 52, 53, 75, 113, 147

J

Jelly jewels 181
jelly. Peach 109

K

kitchen scales 9
Kitty girl cupcakes 156
knick knacks 29

L

Lemonade cake 181
LGBTQI+ 148
liquefying eggs 18

M

macaron vs macaroon 214
macarons
- Aussie gold macarons 110
- Birthday cake macarons 104
- Catching feelings macarons 183
- colouring 18
- Divas getting money macarons 186
- Forbidden doughnut macarons 106–7
- French method 214
- Highway unicorn macarons 71
- Mirror mirror macarons 126
- Peach macarons 109
- Pink print macarons 184
- storing 18
- Stunning brown cow ice-cream macarons 72
- tips and tricks 18–19, 214–5
- troubleshooting 19
- Vanilla macarons 42–4
- Yay! Gay! macarons 162

Magic mushroom cake 102–103
Magic mushrooms 102–3
measuring ingredients 9, 21
measuring tools 21
Midnight galaxy cupcakes 61
Mini chocolate bars 140–1
Mint choc-chip freakshake cupcakes 130–1
Mirror glaze 172–3, 204
Mirror mirror macarons 126
Molasses buttercream 96–7
motivation 53
moulds 22
music 147, 149

N

Neapolitan cupcakes 89
Nicki Star Tip 166–7
No-bake birthday cake cupcakes 207

O

Ombre frosting 212–13
oven temperatures 10
ovens 163

P

paint, Chocolate 72
paint, Gold 124–5
Paris brest cupcakes 83–4
pastry, Choux 83–4
Peach bum cupcakes 64–5
Peach cookies 64–5
Peach jelly 109
Peach macarons 109
photography 26, 53
Pink frosting 156
Pink gelatin bubbles 56–7
Pink princess crowns 154
Pink print macarons 184
piping 13, 22
- piping bags 13, 22
- piping tips 22

Platinum blonde cupcakes 177

R

Rainbow frosting 153
Raspberry frosting 98–9
Raspberry ganache 212–13
Red frosting 153
Red velvet cupcakes 33
reverse-creaming method 34
ribbon stage 18–19
round bulb frosting style 14
Royal icing 106–7

S

Salted caramel cupcakes 86
Salted caramel sauce 50
sauces
- Boozy chocolate sauce 191
- Chocolate sauce 51, 138
- leftovers 214
- Salted caramel sauce 50
- Sugar-free chocolate sauce 136–7
- Vegemite–caramel sauce 110
- White chocolate sauce 191

Schoolin' life cake 212–13
scissors 163
Sea Kween cupcakes 58
signature swirl frosting style 14
Silicone daydream cupcakes 122–3
Silver-star splatter 61
Skin mirror glaze 122–3
social media 52
soft-serve swirl frosting style 14
spatulas 21, 163
Speckled egg macarons cupcakes 201
Speckled eggs 194–5
splatter, Silver-star 61
stand mixer 21
storage 10
Strawberry birthday cake 208–9
Strawberry frosting 96–7
Strawberry ganache 140–1
Striped frosting 98–9, 208–9
Stunning brown cow ice-cream macarons 72
sugar thermometer 18
Sugar-free buttercream frosting 136–7
Sugar-free chocolate sauce 136–7
Sugar-free mint mocha milkshake cupcakes 136–7
Sundae fundae cupcakes 62–3
Swiss meringue buttercream frosting 46
- tips and tricks 12

syrup, Blood 119
syrup, Bloody 122–3

T

Teal ganache drizzle 98–9
The Scran Line 5, 53, 147
tins 25
Tiramisu cupcakes 91
tools and equipment 21–9
trays 25
trimming 10
Turkish delight gel 172–3

U

utensils 29, 163

V

Vanilla cake 37
Vanilla cupcakes 34
Vanilla macarons 42–4
Vegan buttercream frosting 48
Vegan chocolate frosting 78–9
Vegan chocolate raspberry cake 78–9
Vegan cookies and cream cupcakes 77
Vegan frosting 77
video editing 26
Voodoo Halloween cake 124–5

W

Watermelon freakshake cupcakes 134–5
Wedding cake cupcakes 204–5
When macaron met cupcake cupcakes 82
White chocolate ganache 192
White chocolate sauce 191
White chocolate spheres 158–9
White frosting 124–5

Y

Yay! Gay! macarons 162
yoghurt, using 9

THANK YOU

I'd like to give thanks some very important people in my life.

ROB FROM NICKO'S KITCHEN

Rob, you're an amazing mentor to me, and at this point you're basically family. A brother maybe? I don't feel good about calling you my dad. Thanks so much for all the advice that has led to me being able to make a book. I'm so grateful. Also, I'll never get tired of your YouTube conspiracy theories. I fall for them every time (before I come to my senses). We've known each other for 4 years, and while we've never met in person, I'm grateful to call you my friend. Thank you for talking me off the ledge (business-wise) so many times.

TASTEMADE

Tastemade are a social media brand based in LA who have given me amazing career opportunities. I'd like to specifically thank Slim, Olivia and Allie. You guys are incredible. Thank you for giving me the opportunity to do the job I love.

DAN

You're an amazing friend. I'm grateful to be able to pick up the phone and bounce things off you, or to catch up with you and Rob. It helps me more than you know. Thank you for being an incredible friend.

KRYSELDA

My number one fan. From the very beginning, you have believed in me and you've inspired me to keep being myself and to laugh. You're my Filipina Beyoncé and Cardi B combined in one. I'm Onika. Always.

ELISE FROM MY CUPCAKE ADDICTION

Elise, you're amazing. I've told you this a thousand times, but I don't know how you do what you do and keep raising a family. You're truly an inspiration to me in so many ways. Above everything though, your kindness and generosity is what I value the most.

JELL RADFORD

You're part of my story. You were the first person I came out to, the person who showed me love and acceptance at a time when I felt the most vulnerable in my life, and who helped me jump-start the journey to becoming the fierce KWEEN I am today with no f$$$s to give about what anyone thinks of me. Thank you.

NOULA – MY SISTER.

Nobody makes me feel more myself and more accepted than you do. Your story inspires me. Also, is someone cutting onions?

TIM, JONNY, ILLIANNA AND NANDA

You're acknowledged. Also, ily a trilly.

TO MY THREE LITTLE NEPHEWS

Harvey, the little afstraleso wog who is truly our joy. Finny – the smile monster, and Edison the fighter. You have brought so much joy to our family. I can't wait for you to get older so we can bake lots of yummy things together.

LAURA VITALE

We've never met, you most likely don't know who I am, but I have to say ... You inspired me to start my YouTube journey. The Scran Line started as a food blog. Then I discovered you on YouTube and that was it for me. I was obsessed with your recipe videos. I've taken inspiration from the way you talk about food, your relationship with it, your story, everything! You have inspired me more than you'll probably ever know. If i was in a room with you and Beyoncé I'm not sure who I would fangirl over more. Thank you for being such a huge inspiration to me.

MAGGIE MAGGIE MAGGIE

You're already in the book. But you know how much I love you. I don't know what I would do without your giggle and kindness. Thank you so much for being in my life and for showing me an unimaginable amount of patience.

RECIPE TESTERS

Thank you to all the people who generously donated their time and ingredients to testing the recipes in this book. I'm so grateful to you guys, you're amazing and so fun to work with :)

Jess, Candice, Erin, Sara, Rhiannon, Steph, Sophie, Leah, Nathalie, Monique, Annaleis.

ANTHONY

Lastly, I want to thank Anthony.

Anthony, since the day that I met you, you've made me feel like a better version of myself. Someone more rational and less crazy. You've given me amazing advice and perspective and it's been so helpful during one of the most challenging projects I've worked on. You are truly one of the most amazing people I know. Thank you bello. Also #SerrrfBooortt #HellohMbehmbeh #VidjahOfUs.

THANK YOU, FROM A PROFESSIONAL IDIOT TO YOU...

I describe myself as a professional idiot. It's true. I follow the lead of one of my favourite TV office bosses who hilariously terrorises and distracts his entire staff with childish nonsense and pointless meetings about nothing, or spreads rumours about one person, realises that it was a bad idea, so spreads some more rumours about everyone else in the office so that nobody knows what rumours are true. At the end of the day though, he has a heart of gold. Or, as he puts it: 'Would I rather be feared or loved? Both. I want people to be afraid of how much they love me.'

I'm very passionate about what I do, but I was never academic in school. I rarely got an A, but I am clever enough to know who got me here: you guys.

The truth is, guys, I would not be here without you. And, more importantly, this book wouldn't even exist. I've gotten that many emails and comments from you guys over the years asking for a book and you've nagged it into existence, and I thank you for that. Thank you to the people who have supported me throughout the years, first on YouTube and then on Instagram, Facebook and by email. You guys have helped me in so many ways. Let me give you a couple of examples ...

Most of the time I'm a very happy person – I'm doing my dream job after all! But, like everyone, I have some days when I get in a bit of a funk. And, on those days, the emails I get from you guys simply saying 'thank you for making videos' help re-energise me. I love getting those emails. So, to everyone who has taken the time to do that, I'd like to say thank you back!

To everyone who watches my videos on YouTube, Instagram and Facebook, and hits the 'Like' button or comments and tags their friends, thank you.

Lastly, I want to specifically thank three types of people in my audience:

1. People living with a mental illness. It's an unusual group of people to single out, right? First of all, I get what it's like. I have an eating disorder (weird, I know, for someone who makes cupcakes every day for a living!) So, I know what it's like to have an ongoing struggle inside your head that make some days really tough to be happy. If you want to learn more about that, flip over to my coming-out story on page 147–49. One of the things I never expected was that people would write to me and say that my videos have a calming effect on them that helps keep their depression or anxiety in check. I think that's incredible! I want to thank you for being brave enough to share your story with me.

2. Mothers, fathers and grandparents. Another thing I never expected! Ha! One time I got an email from a mother who sent me a photo of her son who didn't look old enough to walk, watching one of my videos on their huge TV and I couldn't stop laughing. I think that's amazing. I get emails from you guys telling me your kids feel inspired by what I do, which is also amazing. I never expected that I'd get the tick of approval from parents, but I'm grateful. My goal is to encourage everyone to get into the kitchen: bake, bond and have fun with their friends and family. The fact that kids are inspired enough by my work to not stare at their screen and bake something sweet instead is incredible.

3. People within the LGBTQI+ community. It's no secret that I'm a flaming homosexual from way back, so I feel blessed that the people who mean so much to me love my work. Initially, The Scran Line was simply about sharing recipes. But, as the audience grew, I felt a responsibility to create a safe and positive space for everyone, especially for my chosen family whose stories and strength inspire me every single day. When I get emails from people telling me their struggles, their coming-out stories or simply thanking me for the work that I do that makes them feel happy, it really fills my heart with so much happiness. So, to everyone who is part of the LGBTQI+ community, thank you for sharing your stories and for inspiring me.

Without all of you, this book wouldn't exist. This book is for you guys.

THE THREE WISE WOMEN

The most important people in my life, who have played a major role in shaping the person I am today, are the women who surround me. More specifically, my yiayia (grandma), my mum and my cupcake fairy godmother and mentor, Maggie.

I want to dedicate this book to you.

TO MY YIAYIA

She would spend all week shopping for her legendary Sunday roast and get up at 4 am every Sunday morning to prepare it for us. She taught me how to do everything with love. Food was the centre of our family because of her, and it's what kept us all together. I miss watching her read her books, her animated storytelling and her amazing food. That's her in the framed photo.

TO MY MUM

She has dedicated her life to being an amazing single mother for her six kids. In my life, my grandma and mum have been my parents and the reason why I have everything I have. My mum is the strongest person I know, and it's because of her that I'm a strong person. Also, a stubborn person. Like, extremely stubborn. My mum has been my biggest supporter and I'm grateful to her for encouraging me to pursue my passion for art. I wouldn't be where I am today without my mum's support, and I'm very grateful to her. My favourite things about my mum are talking to her about food, cooking with her, shopping with her and eating with her. The biggest compliment I can give her is that she's just as amazing at being a yiayia to her grandkids as my yiayia was to me and my brothers and sisters.

TO MAGGIE

Where do I start with Maggie? The first day I met with Maggie it was 4 am on Valentine's Day. After I applied three times to work in a cupcake bakery, Maggie called me and asked me to come in and do a trial. I was greeted by loud '80s pop and a small underground kitchen littered with pink velvet cupcakes as I walked in that morning. She thought, judging by the look of horror on my face, that I would never come back. But I've never seen anyone work as hard as Maggie did that morning, and that's what made me come back. Maggie taught me to never tolerate anything less than perfection in the kitchen, never take anything too seriously, and how to bake amazing cupcakes. The cupcakes you see in this book are the result of a very patient woman who persevered with a professional idiot (me) and spent six months training me to bake something edible. My favourite thing about Maggie is her giggle. If you meet her, it will be yours too.

To my mum, yiayia and Maggie. I love you, and thank you. I am where I am because of you.

Published in 2019 by Hardie Grant Books,
an imprint of Hardie Grant Publishing

Hardie Grant Books (Melbourne)
Building 1, 658 Church Street
Richmond, Victoria 3121

Hardie Grant Books (London)
5th & 6th Floors
52–54 Southwark Street
London SE1 1UN

hardiegrantbooks.com

A catalogue record for this book is available from the National Library of Australia

Sugar Rebels
ISBN 978 1 74379 501 9
10 9 8 7 6 5 4 3 2 1

Managing Editor: Marg Bowman
Project Editor: Anna Collett
Editor: Andrea O'Connor
Design Manager: Jessica Lowe
Internal design: Andy Warren
Typesetter: Megan Ellis
Photographer: Nick Makrides, Armelle Habib
Stylist: Nick Makrides, Karina Duncan
Home Economist: Caitlin Bell
Production Manager: Todd Rechner

Colour reproduction by Splitting Image Colour Studio
Printed in China by Leo Paper Product. LTD